CORRESPONDING
WITH
LEGENDS

CRAIG SIEVERS

BOOKS

Downtown

COFFEE

Auburn, NY

Copyright © 2012 by Craig Sievers

Downtown Books & Coffee
66 Genesee Street
Auburn, NY 13021
downtownbooksandcoffee.com

Cover Design: Ryan Zygarowicz-Bartlett
Cover Photography: Craig Sievers

*To Jack Gregory , Liam Sargent and the
left handed knuckle ball.*

CONTENTS

INTRODUCTION

Dear Reader,

I have always been a baseball fan. Truthfully though, since I was young, I have been more of a fan of the history of the game. On a trip to a flea market when I was eight years old my Grandma Sievers gave me a dime to pick out five cards from the two cent baseball card boxes. Maybe it was because I was young, but it seemed like there was a million cards to sort through to pick out my five.

To this day I remember trying to find the oldest cards I could. I only recall three of the five two decades and change later: a 1957 Topps Hector Lopez, a 1985 Topps Yogi Berra and a 1987 Sportflics Bo Jackson. The Hector Lopez was beat up and cool. The Yogi Berra was, well, Yogi Berra. The Bo Jackson card moved in a batting motion when I turned the card left to right. I was eight after all.

Those cards led to thousands more and my thirst for old baseball cards still has not been slaked. What did change was seven years after my first flea market trip I was introduced to a book with addresses to contact Major Leaguers.

I sent out some of my old cards asking that they might be signed. I waited a few days, not really knowing what to expect. Then I received my first return. It was a 1961 Topps card signed by Hall Of Famer Robin Roberts. I will never part with that card. You always remember your first.

After that I ramped up my stamp use. Stopping at the mail box on my way home from school became the highlight of my day.

Some afternoons I would have one envelope with my name and address in my own hand waiting for me. Some afternoons there were none. Then there were those banner days when there was a pile of self addressed stamped envelopes beckoning for me to discover what they held in store.

It was in one of those envelopes that I made an unexpected find that would turn my passion in a different direction. I sent a card to Roy Sievers. Not only was he the inaugural American League Rookie of the Year in 1949, but he also shares my semi-rare surname. In my note I asked him politely if he would sign my 1955 Topps card of him. As a foot note I asked him if he thought that he and I were related.

I received my card signed beautifully in blue ball point pen. More than that, I received a full page hand written letter from Mr. Sievers telling me that we were not kinfolk, but that he had put forth some effort to find out. He thanked me for my interest and signed the letter "Regards, Roy."

It occurred to me that these men I was writing were actually reading my letters. What's more, they might be willing to write me back. This got me thinking. Instead of getting an autograph on a baseball card, I should start researching the players and ask questions pertinent to their careers. Needless to say, my nose was in the baseball encyclopedia in an instant.

I started sending out letters and asking questions. I have received hundreds of responses over the past decade plus. Some responses have been short and sweet, some long and detailed and some have never come back. For the cost of two stamps I have pulled the lever of the baseball history slot machine and more often than not have come up three cherries. I still look forward to stopping at the mail box.

In this volume are my favorite responses to date. You will see the hand written answers to my questions on one page. On the following page you will find a transcription of the letter (which are often difficult to decipher) and a short bit of biographical information.

I have included replies that mention various Hall of Famers: Lou Gehrig, Branch Rickey, Satchel Paige, Jimmie Foxx, Roberto Clemente, Lefty Grove, "Cool Papa" Bell, Carl Hubbell, Babe Ruth, Ted Williams, Eddie Collins, Joe DiMaggio, Bill Mazeroski, Leo Durocher, Ducky Medwick, Pie Traynor, Mickey Mantle, Josh Gibson, Connie Mack and many, many more.

Also included are responses from Hall of Famers such as Bobby Doerr, Enos Slaughter, George Kell and Brooks Robinson. There are All Stars, World Series winners and losers, pitchers who hurled no hitters, sluggers who hit grand slams, fellows who spent their whole lives in the game, others who lasted just a few contests.

There is a letter from the pitcher who gave up Babe Ruth's record tying 59th home run in 1927, the 18 year old who hit a homer off of Satchel Paige in Yankee Stadium, the player who inspired one of the greatest baseball movies of all time, the winner of the first televised game in 1939, a Hall of Famer's son, the college coach who cut a young John Grisham, an expecting father who hit a home run after hearing of the healthy arrival of his first born along with dozens more.

It is interacting with the past in a very old fashioned way. If you are an enthusiast of the history of the game of baseball, I am hoping the following pages will bring you a fraction of the anticipation and interest that I felt as I was peeling open the envelopes.

Regards,

Craig

1961 Topps Robin Roberts

1955 Topps Roy Sievers

TEAMMATES

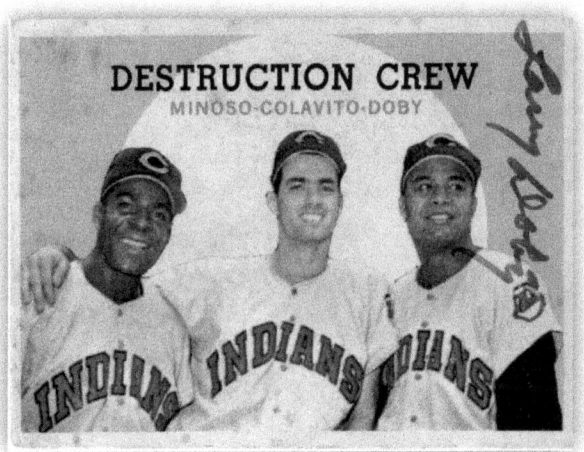

Bill "Moose" Skowron on Roger Maris:

A Great Player & A great Guy

Moose

Al Milnar on player/manager Lou Boudreau:

not many players under. Boudreau
resented him being manager. old or young
he had their respect. He was intelligent besides
being a great short stop (Hall of Fame) A gentleman off
the field. Wish him good health in his lifetime

Al Milnar
Cleveland
Indians

1936-38 To 46   *SERVICE*
1944-45

Tommy Byrne on achievement:

Being healthy enough to wear the
Yankee uniform —   *Tommy Byrne*

Carl Erskine on Jackie Robinson:

Hi Craig

I was fortunate to play with a great team — several Hall of Famers. Jackie was a high spirited competitor and helped us win six National League Championships in years 1947 to 1956.

Jackie & I were team mates for nine seasons - (I missed 1947) — We were also good friends off the field and often visited schools, hospitals and youth groups. We remained good friends until he died young in about 1973 —

Regards,

Carl Erskine
Dodgers 1948 -1959

Hi Craig,

I was fortunate to play with a great team-several Hall of Famers. Jackie was a high spirited competitor and helped us win six National League Championships in years 1947 to 1956.

Jackie & I were teammates for nine seasons. (I missed 1947)- We were also good friends off the field and often visited schools, hospitals and youth groups.

We remained good friends until he died young in about 1973.

Regards,
Carl Erskine
Dodgers 1948-1959

Carl Erskine pitched his entire 12 year career for the Dodgers, 10 in Brooklyn and two in Los Angeles. He pitched in one All Star game and in 1953 led the league in winning percentage with a won/loss record of 20-6 good for a .769 mark.

Erskine, or "Oisk" as he was known to Brooklyn fans, had a stellar 122-78 regular season record over his career. He was a member of five National League pennant winning Dodger clubs including one World Series winner. "Oisk" set a World Series record with 14 strike outs in game 3 in 1953. That record stood until it was broken by another Dodger, Sandy Koufax a decade later.

Jackie Robinson had few allies when he broke the color barrier, Carl Erskine was one of his first and proved to be most loyal.

Charlie Devens on Lou Gehrig:

Dear Craig -

    ,I did not know Gehrig very well, but I certainly was glad that he was on my team and not against me.

        Good Luck -

           Charlie Devens.

CHARLIE DEVENS
NEW YORK YANKEES – PITCHER   1932

Dear Craig,

I did not know Gehrig very well, but I certainly was glad that he was on my team and not against me.

Good Luck,
Charlie Devens

Charles Devens was born in Milton Massachusetts in 1910. He attended Harvard University and pitched for their nine. Devens was a top prospect for the New York Yankees when he was called up for one start in 1932. He hurled a two run six hit complete game. In 1933 and 1934 combined Devens pitched 15 games with nine starts. He won four and lost three.

Many players have had short careers for various reasons. Devens' reason had nothing to do with ineffectiveness or injury. Charlie Devens fell in love with the daughter of a wealthy Boston businessman and proposed her marriage. His would be father in law refused to have his daughter wed a baseball player. Big League baseball in the 1930's was not considered a solid profession.

So Charlie Devens got married and his Major League career came to an end. He chose love over the mound. With his Harvard education, Devens went on to become a successful businessman in Boston.

Vern Law on Roberto Clemente:

Dear Craig,

I do think over Era was the Golden age of baseball and feel privileged to have played in the 70's & 60's. We didn't make much money but had a lot of fun, and I sure don't like the way the game has gone these past few years.

It was a thrill to have played with Roberto, he was a great player and real competitor, probably deserves more credit than he's gotten.

He was overshadowed by Mays & Aaron during that time but he could play right with them. He played the outfield as good or better than Aaron, not Mays. He didn't hit the Home runs that either of them hit nor did he steal the bases they did, but he could do everything in the outfield that they did and more.

He was a good friend with a very infectious smile and a good sense of humor.

Thanks for your interest.

Vern Law

Dear Craig,

I do think our era was the Golden Age of baseball and feel privileged to have played in the 50's and 60's. We didn't make much money but had a lot of fun, and I sure don't like the way the game has gone these past few years.

It was a thrill to have played with Roberto, he was a great player and a real competitor. Probably deserves more credit than he's gotten.

He was overshadowed by Mays and Aaron, during that time but he could play right with them. He played the outfield as good or better than Aaron, not Mays.

He didn't hit the home runs that either of them hit nor did he steal the bases they did, but he could do everything in the outfield that they could and more.

He was a good friend with a very infectious smile and a good sense of humor.

Thanks for your interest.
Vern Law

Vern Law pitched his entire 16 season career for the Pittsburgh Pirates. His lone All Star nod came during the World Series winning season of 1960. That year he went 20-9 with 18 complete games earning him the Cy Young Award. Law won the first National League Comeback Player of the Year Award in 1965. That same year he won the Lou Gehrig Award.

Enos Slaughter on the "Gas House Gang":

Craig.

We had youth, dedication and
we all pulled together pitching
speed and enough power to win

Best Wishes

Enos Slaughter

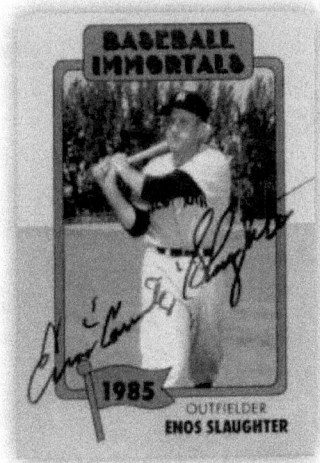

Craig,

We had youth, determination and we all pulled together pitching speed and enough power to win.

Best Wishes
Enos Slaughter

Enos Bradsher "Country" Slaughter was born in Roxboro North Carolina in 1916. He began his Big League career in 1938 with the St. Louis Cardinals. In the following 19 seasons Slaughter was named to 10 National League All Star teams. Slaughter was a member of five World Series championship teams: twice with the Cardinals and later thrice with the New York Yankees.

While with the "Gas House Gang" Cardinals of the early 1940's Slaughter was a member of two World Series championship squads. His first championship team was in 1942. Separated by four years in the Armed Forces during World War II "Country" returned state side to be a driving force on the '46 Champs. Shaking off the rust of his four year layoff, Slaughter led the National League in runs batted in during the regular season with 130.

Enos Slaughter is perhaps best remembered for what he did in Game 7 of the 1946 World Series against the Boston Red Sox. In the eighth inning with Slaughter on first, Harry "The Hat" Walker hit a single. Slaughter went from 1st to home and slid in safe with what would be Series winning run. The play became known as "The Mad Dash" and has since lived in lore as one of the greatest personal efforts World Series history.

Bobby Shantz on the Yankees:

Craig,
Playing for the Yankees was the greatest four years of my life. I don't think they're will ever be a ball club like the Yankees of the 50's. Today's Yankees are nothing like Berra, Mantle, Ford, Skowron, Bauer and Richardson.

Sincerely,
Bobby Shantz

BOBBY SHANTZ
NEW YORK YANKEES   PITCHER

Craig,

    Playing for the Yankees was the greatest four years of my life. I don't think there will ever be a ball club like the Yankees of the 50's. Today's Yankees are nothing like Berra, Mantle, Ford, Skowron, Bauer and Richardson.

    Sincerely,
    Bobby Shantz

Robert Clayton Shantz was a side arm throwing lefty with a wicked curve ball. During the first quarter of his 16 season career he helped lead the Athletics' revival in Philadelphia. While in Philly Shantz was a two time American League All Star. In 1952 he won 24 games and lost 7 good for a league leading .774 winning percentage. Those statistics led to him earning an American League Most Valuable Player nod for the 1952 season.

As a member of the A's in the 1952 All Star game Shantz was called on to pitch the final inning. With the Mid Summer Classic on the line he struck out three prominent batsmen: Whitey Lockman, Jackie Robinson and Stan "The Man" Musial.

Shantz went on to win two World Series with the New York Yankees in 1957 and 1960. In 1957 he was named to his third American League All Star team; however he did not make an appearance in the contest.

Bobby Shantz fielded his position as well as anyone did during his era. He won eight Gold Gloves for his fielding prowess around the mound. The first Gold Glove he won was the first ever awarded to a pitcher.

Mahlon Duckett on the Negro Leagues:

May 19th, 1997

Hello Craig:

Nice hearing from you and to learn of your interest in the former Negro Leagues plus their players. You asked about some of my greatest thrills in Baseball, well Craig it was such a great thrill to have been able to have played in the Negro Leagues for eleven seasons (1940-1950) inclusive. I can tell you the greatest thrill of all as a player. In 1941 before about 50,000 fans in Yankee Stadium I hit a game winning home run off of the great Satchell Paige. I was only eighteen years old at the time so you know that is something I shall never forget. I had a good career all in all, I was known for my speed and defense and also had a strong ball. I always hit either first or second in our line up. I couldn't tell you exactly what my career batting average was but I did alright. 1946 thru 1950 my figures was great as they where all 300 plus (batting average). I also had the pleasure to have played with or against nine (9) of the Negro Players who are a the deal of fame. Players like Josh Gibson, Satchell Paige, Buck Leonard, Cool "Papa" Bell, Ray Dandridge, Oscar Charleston, Leon Day, Monte Irvin, and Judy Johnson.

Sincerely,
Mahlon Duckett

Hello Craig:

Nice hearing from you and to learn of your interest in the former Negro Leagues plus the players. You asked about some of my greatest thrills in baseball. Well Craig it was such a great thrill to have been able to have played in the Negro Leagues for eleven seasons (1940-1950) inclusive. I can tell you the greatest thrill of all as a player. In 1941 before about 50,000 fans in Yankee Stadium I hit a game winning home run off of the great Satchel Paige. I was only eighteen years old at the time so you know that is something I will never forget. I had a good career all in all. I was known for my speed and defense and also had a strong ball. I always hit either first or second in the lineup. I couldn't tell you exactly what my career batting average was but I did alright. 1946 through 1950 my figures were great as they were all over .300 yrs (batting average). I also had the pleasure to have played with or against nine (9) of the Negro Players who are in the Hall of Fame. Players like Josh Gibson, Satchel Paige, Buck Leonard, "Cool Papa" Bell, Ray Dandridge, Oscar Charleston, Leon Day, Monte Irvin, and Judy Johnson.

Sincerely,
Mahlon Duckett

Mahlon Duckett began his professional career at the age of 17. He was the Negro National League Rookie of the Year in 1940. Duckett played for the Philadelphia Stars from 1940 through 1949. He spent his final year with the Homestead Grays in 1950 as integration became prominent in the Major Leagues causing the Negro Leagues to fade.

Leo Nonnenkamp on Grove and Foxx:

GROVE WAS ABOUT TO WIND UP HIS CAREER. HAD
MELLOWED. ALWAYS PITCHED WELL WHEN CALLED UPON,
WAS ESPECIALLY PLEASANT WITH THE ROOKIES.

FOXX - TEAMATES ENJOYED CALLING HIM "THE BEAST"
AFTER HE HIT ONE OF HIS TAPE-MEASURED DRIVES.
COMING BACK TO THE BENCH, AFTER ONE OF THE DRIVES,
HE WOULD JUST "GRUNT" AND SMILE. NO HIGH FIVES IN
THOSE DAYS - EVERYONE KNEW WHEN THEY WERE DOING WELL.

GOOD LUCK TO YOU,

Leo Nonnenkamp

Grove was about to wind up his career. Had mellowed. Always pitched well when called upon. Was especially pleasant with the rookies.

Foxx- Teammates enjoyed calling him "The Beast". After he hit one of his tape measured drives. Coming back to the bench, after one of the drives, he would just "grunt and smile". No high fives in those days. Everyone knew when they were doing well.

Good luck to you
Leo Nonnenkamp

Leo William "Red" Nonnenkamp was born in Saint Louis Missouri in 1910. In 1933 he played one game for the Pittsburgh Pirates. From 1938 through 1940 Nonnenkamp played 154 contests as an outfielder for the Boston Red Sox. In 1938 he batted .283 in 180 plate appearances.

"Lefty" Grove hurled for 17 seasons in the Big Leagues for the Philadelphia Athletics and the Boston Red Sox. He won 300 games, was named to six American League All Star teams and was elected to the Hall of Fame in 1947. In the seasons that Grove and Nonnenkamp were teammates, Grove won 36 games and was named to two All Star squads. Jimmie Foxx played 20 seasons in the Majors and during his time was a feared slugger. Throughout his two decades he belted 534 home runs and was named to nine American League All Star teams. 1951 brought his induction into the Hall. When Foxx and Nonnenkamp shared the field, Foxx belted 121 home runs and was voted to the American League All Star team all three seasons.

Charlie Wagner on the Red Sox:

Dear Craig,

One of my biggest thrills, when I made it to the "big leagues" and enjoyed the the fact that I played with, and against some real hall of fame players, and I also roomed with "Ted Williams" for six years Foxx, Cronin, Doer, Lefty Grove were the fellows I played with, it was a great era of Hall of Fame I played against too.

It was an enjoyable life and I am still in the game. I've been with the "Red Sox" 63 yrs as a scout and pitching instructor.

Good luck and good health —

Sincerely

Charlie Wagner —

Dear Craig,

One of my biggest thrills, when I made it to the "big leagues" and enjoyed the fact that I played with, and against some real hall of fame players, and also roomed with 'Ted Williams' for six years. Foxx, Cronin, Doerr, Lefty Grove were the fellows I played with it was a great era of Hall Of Famers I played against too.

It was an enjoyable life and I am still in the game. I've been with the 'Red Sox' 63 years as a scout and pitching instructor.

Good luck and good health-
Sincerely
Charlie Wagner

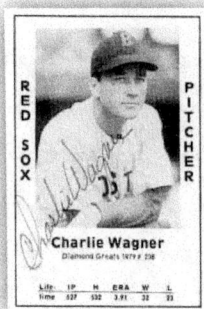

Charlie Wagner pitched six seasons for the Boston Red Sox starting in 1938. In 1941 he had 12 wins and followed that with 14 victories in 1942. In six seasons Wagner had an overall record of 32 wins and 23 losses all with the Red Sox, but his baseball career was far from over.

Wagner went on to hold several positions within the Red Sox organization. He started as a scout, a roving minor league pitching instructor, and even into his 90's he kept tabs on prospects. In 1970 Wagner was the pitching coach for the Boston Red Sox. Summing the years of his pitching career, his years as a coach, and his years as a scout, Charlie Wagner spent 73 years with the Boston Red Sox.

Gil McDougald on Mantle and Maris:

Dear Craig –
The 50's & early 60's was a great
time to play major league ball; & still better
to play for so many winning Yankee teams. All
the above were great players along with D.Mag,
Berra, Rizzuto, Bauer, Woodling, Collins, Brown & a
great pitching staff of Raschi, Reynolds & Lopat.

Sincerely
Gil

GIL McDOUGALD
2nd-3rd base N. Y. YANKEES

Dear Craig-

 The 50's & early 60's were a great time to play major league ball & still better to play for so many winning Yankee teams. All the above were great players along with DiMag, Berra, Rizzuto, Bauer, Woodling, Collins, Bauer & a great pitching staff of Raschi, Reynolds & Lopat.

   Sincerely,
   Gil

 Gil McDougald manned the infield for a decade for the New York Yankees starting in 1951. That 1951 season garnered him American League Rookie of the Year honors. During that time the Bombers appeared in eight Fall Classics, winning five. McDougald was named to six American League All Star teams playing in four of the games. He led the league in triples with nine in 1957 and fielding percentage in 1955 with a .985 clip. He belted 112 home runs and batted in 576 runs during his career.

 In 1957 through pure poor luck, McDougald hit a piercing line drive that struck Cleveland's prodigy hurler Herb Score in the eye. At the time Score was an incredible ascending talent, having won 16 games in '55 and 20 in 1956. To his credit, as it was no fault of his own, McDougald vowed that he would quit the Major Leagues if Herb Score went blind due to his line drive. Score did not go blind, but McDougald went deaf after being hit by a pitch. After his playing career Gil became an advocate for the hearing impaired.

Elden Auker on his Hall of Fame Friends:

Dear Craig:

I consider myself to be very fortunate, to have had the opportunity to play Professional Baseball in the Major Leagues for 10 years. I have many fond memories of our 1934, 1935 American League Championships and the two World Series, winning the Worlds Series in 1935. Many others too numerous to mention. The best of all experiences, was the privilege and Honor to have played with and against many great Gentlemen of the game, namely, Babe Ruth, Lou Gehrig, Charley Gehringer & Hank Greenberg, Jimmy Foxx, Ted Williams, Lefty Grove on an on and on. Those who made the game great and all of these great men were my friends. For that I will be forever Grateful. I was very lucky.

God Bless

Elden Auker

Dear Craig,

I consider myself to be very fortunate, to have had the opportunity to play professional baseball in the Major Leagues for 10 years. I have many fond memories of our 1934-1935 American League Championships and the two World Series, winning the World Series in 1935. Many others too numerous to mention. The best of all experiences, was the privilege and honor to have played with and against many great gentlemen of the game, namely, Babe Ruth, Lou Gehrig, Charley Gehringer, Hank Greenburg, Jimmy Foxx, Ted Williams, Lefty Grove on and on and on. Those who made the game great and all of these great men were my friends. For that I will be forever grateful. I was very lucky.

God Bless
Elden Auker

Elden Auker was born in Norcatur, Kansas in 1910. He went on to pitch a decade's worth of seasons in the Majors for three teams. In 1935 he was a member of the Detroit Tigers squad that was victorious in the World Series. That year, in the regular season, he led the American League in winning percentage with an 18 win and 7 loss record good for a .720 mark. Somehow that performance did not earn him an American League All Star nod. His 130-101 career mark was good for a .563 winning percentage.

Auker was a three sport star at Kansas State University. He lettered in football, basketball and baseball. A 2nd team All American quarterback, Auker turned down a $6,000.00 offer from the Chicago Bears. The legendary Bronko Nagurski visited the Kansas State campus in Manhattan Kansas to try to convince Auker to accept the Bears' proposal. As it turned out even the "Galloping Ghost" could not dissuade Auker from pitching for the Tigers.

Don Gutteridge on the "Gas House Gang":

Dear Craig:

If you can imagine yourself as a "farm boy" from the country and walking into a clubhouse full of super stars with your mouth agap and admiring all of them and wondering how they are going to except me – then you know how I felt.

I was soon made to feel at home and was accepted. Then I knew I must excel or some one would take my place. I was lucky that I got off on right foot and it gave me incentive to excel better.

I really enjoyed being there. They were great bunch of fun loving athletes that had fun but when they stepped on playing field they were All Business and they were out to beat the opponents. They would do it any way they could.

No all played ready for the sheer joy of playing, winning and enjoyment to fans. I loved every minute I was there.

Don Gutteridge

Dear Craig,

If you can imagine yourself as a "farm boy" from the country and walking into a clubhouse full of super stars with your mouth agape and admiring all of them and wondering how they are going to except me-then you know how I felt.

I was soon made to feel at home and was accepted. Then I knew I must excel or someone would take my place. I was lucky that I got off on the right foot and it gave me incentive to excel better.

I really enjoyed being there. They were a bunch of fun loving athletes that had fun but when they stepped on the playing fields they were all business and they were out to beat the opponents. They would do it any way they could.

We all played really for the sheer joy of playing, winning and enjoyment of the fans. I loved every minute I was there.

Don Gutteridge

Don Gutteridge played 12 years in the Big Leagues five with the "Gas House Gang" Cardinals. Unfortunately, he did not get to enjoy the World Series success with the Cards. He actually was on the St. Louis Browns and on the losing side of the only all St. Louis World Series in 1944. He also played for Boston when they made the World Series in 1946.

AT THE PLATE

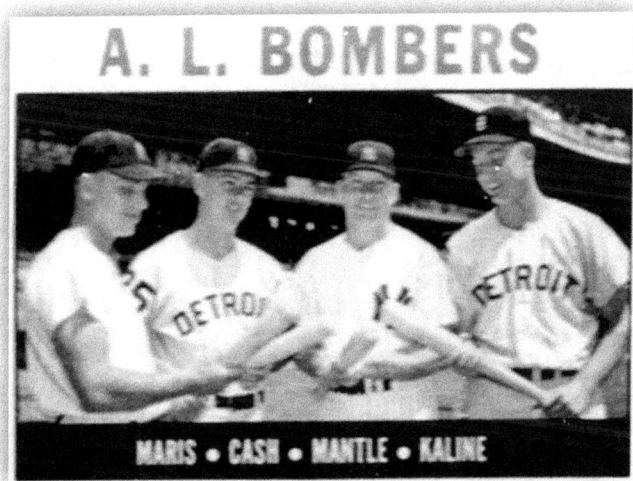

A. L. BOMBERS

MARIS • CASH • MANTLE • KALINE

Johnny Sturm on his greatest thrill:

HITTING SAFELY IN ALL THE GAMES OT
THE '41 SERIES.

Johnny Sturm

Woody Jensen on a great day:

In St. Louis, year 1935 era, playing the St. Louis
Cardinals, hit two home runs off Dizzy Dean - Hall
of Fame pitcher

"Woody Jensen

Stan Lopata on his batting stance:

Dear Craig:

Roger Hornsby had nothing to do with
me changing my batting stance, I did that I
my own. The only thing he suggested to me is
any time or swing the bat get a piece of the ball,
not necessary a base hit, but a piece of the ball and
that's what I started to do. I changed my stance
on my own.

Gil Coan on his first homer and a Presidential baseball:

Dear Craig,

On 6/30/1946 in a game in Fenway Park Boston, batting against left hander Earl Johnson, I hit a high curve ball from him into our bull pen.

Jake Early, our bull pen catcher caught the ball and brought it to me in the club house after the game.

I still have the ball.

Also have a ball that Pres Truman threw out Opening day in 1948 in Washington. He signed the ball for me.

One of my sons when he was 8 yrs old had the ball in our front yard years later when I came home from the office. He and his playmates had a game with it. Signature is still legible but barely.

Sincerely
Gil Coan

Dear Craig,

On 6/30/1946 in a game in Fenway Park Boston, hitting against left hander Earl Johnson, I hit a high curve ball from him into our bull pen.

Jake Early, our bull pen catcher caught the ball and brought it to me in the club house after the game.

I still have the ball.

Also have a ball that Pres. Truman threw out Opening Day in 1948 in Washington. He signed the ball for me.

One of my sons when he was 8 yrs old had the ball in our front yard years later when I came home from the office. He and his playmates had a game with it. Signature is still legible but barely.

Sincerely,
Gil Coan

In 1922 Gilbert Coan was born in Monroe, North Carolina. In 1945 Coan was named the Minor League Player of the Year by the Sporting News while playing in the Southern Association. The following season Coan began his eleven season Major League career roaming the outfield for four different clubs. He spent a majority of his time, eight seasons, with the Washington Senators.

In 1951 Coan pulled off the rare feat of belting two triples in a single inning. Only four other men in the long history of the Big Leagues have done the same.

Gus Suhr with help from his daughter:

My dad's greatest thrill:
 Opening day 1940 Phillies vs.
Giants. Carl Hubbell pitching. Suhr
hits a home run in the 8th inning
two men on, score was Giants -1,
Phillies -0. Homer brought score
to 3-1. This appeared in News
Reels the next day throughout
America.
  Best wishes
  Gus Suhr Pgh Pirate 1930-39
           Phila Phillies 1939-40

"GUS" SUHR

My dad's greatest thrill:

Opening day 1940 Phillies vs. Giants. Carl Hubbell pitching. Suhr hits a home run in the 8th inning two men on, score was Giants- 1 Phillies-0. Homer brought the score to 3-1. This appeared in News Reels the next day throughout America.

Best wishes,
Gus Suhr Pbgh Pirates 1930-39
Phila Phillies 1939-40

Born in 1906 San Francisco, August Richard "Gus" Suhr was a mainstay for the Pittsburgh Pirates at 1st base for a decade beginning in 1930. He set the record for games played by a Pirates first baseman that stands after seven decades. Suhr led the National League in games played five straight seasons from 1932 through 1936. Twice he topped the 100 RBI mark and he accumulated 818 for his 11 season career. In 5176 career at bats Suhr had 1446 base knocks good for a .276 average. 1936 was his finest over all offensive season. That season Suhr scored 111 runs, batted in 118, hit .312, and was a member of the National League All Star team. An athletic 1st baseman, Suhr legged out 114 triples against jogging the bases for 84 home runs.

His total of 17 home runs his rookie year of 1930 was no fluke. In 1929 he made the most of his final year in the minor leagues. Suhr hit .381, slugged 51 home runs and plated an amazing 177 runs batted in.

John Miles on 11 Home Runs in 11 straight games:

HELLO CRAIG!
 YES I HAD AN AMAZING BASE BALL CAREER. PLAYING
ALONG AND WITH BASE BALL STARS IN THE NEGRO LEAGUE
TO NAME A FEW. JACKIE ROBINSON, SATCHEL PAIGE, JOSH GIBSON
HANK AARON, ERNIE BANKS, AND MONTE IRVIN. WAS A GREAT
EXPERIENCE. WE THE PLAYERS DID NOT MAKE A 'LOT' OF MONEY
BUT HAD THE TEARS AND JOY AS WE PLAYED THE GAME.
 NOW HITTING HOME RUNS AND WINNING BALL GAME'S WAS MY
GAME. THE STREAK OF HITTING "11" HOME RUNS IN "11" STRAIGHT
BALL GAMES WAS NOT PLAN. IT JUST HAPPEN, I HAD NO
IDEA THIS WAS GOING ON. I CAME TO BAT IN EACH GAME
TRYING TO GET A BASE HIT AND GET ON BASE FOR THE NEXT
BATTER. BUT SEEING THE BALL AS I WAS, AND SWINGING
FOR DISTANCE THATS WHAT BROUGHT ABOUT A STREAK.
OTHER WORDS I HAD MY EYE ON THE BALL, YOU CANNOT
HIT IT, IF YOU DO NOT SEE IT. "OK"

                    THANK YOU FOR WRITING

                        John "Mule" Miles

WITH OUT THOSE MEMORIES OF THE PAST
THERE CAN BE NO DREAMS OF GREATNESS
IN THE FUTURE.

JOHN 'MULE' MILES.
ALLEN & GINTER'S
BROOKLYN 2007 NEW YORK

Hello Craig;

   Yes I had an amazing baseball career. Playing along with Baseball stars in the Negro League to name a few; Jackie Robinson, Satchel Paige, Josh Gibson, Hank Aaron, Ernie Banks and Monte Irvin was a great experience. We the players did not make a lot of money but had the tears and joy as we played the game.

   Now hitting home runs and winning ball games was my game. The streak of hitting "11" home runs in "11" straight ball games was not plan[ned]. It just happen[ned]. I had no idea this was going on. I came to bat in each game trying to get a base hit and get on base for the next batter. But seeing the ball as I was and swinging for distance that's what brought about a streak.

   Other words I had my eye on the ball. You cannot hit it, if you do not see it. "ok"

   Thank you for writing
   John "Mule" Miles

   Without those memories of the past there can be no dreams of greatness in the future.

John Miles was a Tuskegee Airman. He began his Negro League career in 1945 with the Chicago American Giants. In 1948 he led the Negro American League in home runs with 27. Miles nickname, "Mule" originated from manager Candy Jim Taylor who after Miles connected on two home runs in one game commented, "You hit like a mule kicks!" He finished his career in the integrated Gulf Coast League with the Laredo Apaches in 1951.

Andy Pafko on a Grand Slam for Mom:

Hi Craig:
I've had a lot of thrills in the major leagues. Played in 4 World Series – 4 All Star games – all big thrills. But my biggest thrill was in 1945 when I played with the Chicago Cubs. My mother never saw me play in the major leagues. With her watching me play for the 1st time – I hit a grand slam home run against Pittsburgh. That was her only game she saw me play. She passed away later. To me that was my biggest thrill

Andy Pafko

Hi Craig,

I've had a lot of thrills in the major leagues. Played in 4 World Series- 4 All Star Games- all big thrills.

But my biggest thrill was in 1945 when I played with the Chicago Cubs. My mother never saw me play in the major leagues.

With her watching me play for the 1st time- I hit a grand slam home run against Pittsburgh.

That was her only game she saw me play. She passed away later.

To me that was my biggest thrill.

Andy Pafko

Andy Pafko is best remembered in some circles as the player pictured on card #1 of the inaugural mainstream Topps baseball card set in 1952. Back in the 50's, kids collected baseball cards in numeric order and rubber banded them together damaging the first and last cards in the set. Because of that, the 1952 Topps Andy Pafko #1 is valued at up to $5,000 in near mint condition.

On the field Pafko was valuable as well. He played the outfield for 17 seasons in the Big Leagues. He was the only native Wisconsin to be a member of the Milwaukee Braves that defeated the vaunted New York Yankees in the 1957 World Series. His four All Star seasons all came with the Chicago Cubs from 1947 through 1950. Throughout his tenure Pafko accumulated 1796 hits, 213 of which were homers.

Walt Dropo on his career thrills:

Craig: One of my biggest Thrills
in baseball was being named
to the 1950 All Star Game
Also being named as the
Rookie of the Year 1950
Another thrill was when
I set the record
"12 Consecutive hits"

July 15th 1952

Regards
Walt Dropo

Craig:

> *One of my biggest thrills in baseball was being named to the 1950 All Star Game.*
>
> *Also being named as the Rookie of the Year in 1950.*
>
> *Another thrill was when I set the record "12 consecutive hits"*
>
> *July 15th 1952*

> *Regards,*
> *Walt Dropo*

Walter Dropo was born in Moosup Connecticut in 1923. Dropo went from his parents' farm to the University of Connecticut.

At UConn Dropo was a three sport star. Besides excelling on the diamond he was a star on the grid iron and the hard wood. Dropo at 6'5" and 220 lbs. was drafted 4th overall in the first round of the1947 National Basketball Association draft by the Providence Steamrollers. The year prior, he was drafted by the Chicago Bears in the 9th round of the National Football League draft.

Walt Dropo chose baseball and had a 13 season career. His finest seasons were with the Red Sox and the Detroit Tigers from 1950 to 1953. For his 13 season Major League tenure Dropo hit .270 with 152 dingers and 704 runs batted in.

Howie Schultz on being traded:

Hi Craig,

I had my biggest thrill during the 1947 season after I had been traded to the Phillies from the Dodgers. In a game against the Dodgers at Brooklyn with my mother and father in attendance I hit a grand slam off Vic Lombardi to win the game for the Phillies. My parents being there made it very special.

Sorry about the slow response. You caught me in our move from our winter place in Florida back to Minnesota.

Best wishes,

Howie Schultz

Hi Craig,

I had my biggest thrill during the 1947 season after I had been traded to the Phillies from the Dodgers. In a game against the Dodgers at Brooklyn with my mother and father in attendance I hit a grand slam off Vic Lombardi to win the game for the Phillies. My parents being there made it very special.

Sorry about the slow response. You caught me in our move from our winter place in Florida back to Minnesota.

Best wishes,
Howie Schultz

Howard Henry "Stretch" Schultz was born in 1922 in St. Paul Minnesota. He played 1st base for six seasons on three teams in the Majors. The trade he refers to in his response was the one that the Dodgers made to make room to call up a prized prospect from Montreal; one Jack Roosevelt Robinson. During his career Schultz blasted 24 home runs.

At six foot six inches tall, "Steeple" Schultz moved on to hard wood after his Big League career. In four NBA seasons he averaged 5.3 points per game. Schultz played for three teams; The Anderson Packers, The Fort Wayne Pistons and the Minneapolis Lakers. His move from the Majors to the Association proved to be a wise one. Howie Schultz was a member of two National Basketball Association Minneapolis Lakers championship teams.

George Hausmann on his biggest thrill:

my biggest thrill in the majors was over a 3 day period. In June '45 we played and won both games of a double header on a Sunday in Philadelphia. I got 6 hits in 8 at bats. After an off day on Monday, we played Pittsburg in a double-header on Tues. at the Polo Grounds. I was 7 for 8 in the 2 games, highlighted by driving in the tying and winning runs in the bottom of the ninth on a 2 out and 3-2 count against Preacher Roe; final score 3 to 2. 13 hits in 16 times at bat jumped my B.A. over 300 at the time

Geo. Hausmann

GEORGE HAUSMANN

My biggest thrill in the majors was over a 3 day period. In June '45 we played and won both games of a double header on a Sunday in Philadelphia. I got 6 hits in 8 at bats. After an off day on Monday we played Pittsburg in a double header on Tues. at the Polo Grounds. I was 7 for 8 in 2 games, highlighted by driving in the tying and winning runs in the bottom of the ninth on a 2 out and 3-2 count against Preacher Roe; final score 3 to 2. 13 hits in 16 times at bat jumped my B.A. over .300 at the time.

Geo. Hausmann

George Hausmann was born in St. Louis, Missouri in 1916. At 5'5" tall and weighing in at 145 pounds the diminutive Hausmann took over second base duties when Mickey Witek joined the Service in 1944. During the 1944 and '45 seasons he was the Giants regular second baseman. In 1945 Hausmann played in all 154 regular season contests for New York.

In 1946 Hausmann was recruited to play in Mexico and in doing so was suspended from the Big Leagues. The ban on Big Leaguers who jumped to the Mexican League was lifted in 1949 and Hausmann returned to the Giants. He played 16 games in the '49 season.

From 1938 to 1956 George Hausmann played professional baseball. Other than his 301 games with the Giants, he toiled away in the minor leagues. After retiring from the field, Hausmann managed for several seasons in the minors.

Bob Kennedy on his first Home Run:

Hi Craig,

My first H.R. was against Lefty Grove in Boston – Grove was much past his prime I hit a 3-2 pitch leading off the game, I did not know it was a H.R. – until the 3rd base Coach told one, as I was running the Bases. However, it was the only run we got that day. He beat us 4-1 in Boston. I was just 19 at the time

Thank You for Your interest.

God Bless
Bob Kennedy

Hi Craig,

> *My first H.R. was against Lefty Grove in Boston. Grove was much past his prime. I hit a 3-2 pitch leading off the game, I did not know it was a H.R. until the 3rd base coach told me as I was running the bases. However, it was the only run we got that day. He beat us 4-1 in Boston. I was just 19 at the time.*
>
> *Thank you for your interest.*

> *God Bless*
> *Bob Kennedy*

Bob Kennedy played outfield and 3rd base for 16 seasons in the Majors. Throughout his career he belted 63 homers and plated 514 runs. The Chicago White Sox traded Kennedy to the Cleveland Indians half way through the 1948 season. The trade proved fortuitous for Kennedy as the White Sox finished the '48 season in the American League cellar while the Cleveland Indians won the American League Pennant and the World Series.

Kennedy was the manager of the Chicago Cubs from half way through 1963 through midway through the 1965 season. After the Athletics moved from Kansas City to Oakland in 1968 they chose Bob Kennedy as their first manager. In his only season as the A's manager he led them to an 82-80 record, a 20 win improvement from the previous year. Kennedy also served as general manager of the Chicago Cubs from 1977 through 1981. He was also team president during that time.

Brooks Robinson on good advice:

Practice, Practice, Practice
My Dad
Brooks Robins Sr.

Practice, Practice, Practice
       My Dad
       Brooks Robinson

Brooks Calbert Robinson was born in Little Rock Arkansas in 1937. In 1955 Robinson was brought up by the Orioles as an 18 year old 3rd baseman and began a 23 season career in Baltimore.

During his nearly quarter of a century of work with the Orioles Robinson garnered a plethora of awards. 18 seasons he was an American League All Star. After Frank Malzone won the first three, Robinson won 16 consecutive American League Gold Glove Awards for 3rd basemen. In 1964 he was the American League Most Valuable Player.

Brooks Robinson was a member of two World Series Championship clubs, earning the Most Valuable Player Award in the 1970 Series.

Robinson led the American League in fielding percentage for 11 seasons. He is widely regarded as the finest defensive 3rd baseman that has ever walked a diamond. Proving not only his skill but his determination, Robinson played 140 or more contests 17 seasons. He led the American League in games played four times. In 1983 Brooks Robinson was a first ballot inductee into Cooperstown.

Dick Gray on belting the 1st LA Dodger Home run:

Craig

It was a pretty nice day in L.A. that day. The sun was shining and a lot of movie stars were there. There was around 80,000 people that saw the game, and of course it was the Giants against the Dodgers, a bitter rivalry between us. It was around the sixth or seventh inning and the count was 3-0. I hit a foul ball over the left field fence. It was a good feeling. It turned the winning run. That was a long time ago.

God Bless,

Dick Gray

DICK GRAY
ST. LOUIS CARDINALS   INFIELD

Craig,

It was a pretty nice day in L.A. that day. The sun was shining and a lot of movie stars were there. There was around 80,000 people that saw the game, and of course it was the Giants against the Dodgers, a bitter rivalry between us. It was around the sixth or seventh inning and the count was 3-0. I hit a fast ball over the left field fence. It was a good feeling. It turned the winning run. That was a long time ago.

God Bless,
Dick Gray

Richard Benjamin Gray was born in Jefferson Pennsylvania in 1931. He began his tenure in Los Angeles the same year that the Dodgers did, 1958. However, while the Dodgers still reside in The City of Angels, Gray was traded to St. Louis after 21 games of the 1959 season.

Dick Gray spent the rest of the '59 season with the Cardinals and five at bats over nine games in 1960. Over his 124-game career in the Big Leagues Gray had 305 appearances at the plate. He made the most of his .239 average. Of his 73 hits twelve were homers, 6 were triples, 7 were doubles and he plated 41 runs. Also, Gray crossed the plate himself 43 times, including 25 during his rookie season. For good measure, he sprinkled in four stolen bases while being caught only once.

Bill Renna on "The Silent Treatment":

On Aug. 26th 1953 I started in left field for the N.Y. Yankees against Detroit — in Detroit. My wife was in Lenox Hill Hospital in N.Y. expecting our first child.

I had talked to Vi Dickey — Bill Dickey' wife on the phone before I left the Hotel for the ball park that day. My wife Roni was having problems & she informed me she was doing well !!

I had informed the club house man that I may be receiving a phone call — & I wanted to be notified immediately. Just before infield warm up started he called me in for a phone call. It was my wife Roni — and she informed me we had a son — Barry William Renna !!

My first @ bat I hit a home run —.!!! When I returned to the bench they gave mee the silent treatment — no one said anything to me — no hand shakes pats on the back etc.!! Then all of a sudden they all jumped all over me — & gave me a pat pat on the back etc.

That was quite a thrill — & I have never forgotten it !!

Regards,
Bill Renna

On Aug. 26th 1953 I started in left field for the N.Y. Yankees against Detroit- in Detroit. My wife was in Lenox Hill Hospital in N.Y. expecting our first child.

I had talked to Vi Dickey- Bill Dickey's wife on the phone before I left the hotel for the ball park that day. My wife Roni was having problems & she informed me she was doing well!!

I had informed the club house man that I may be receiving a phone call- & I wanted to be notified immediately. Just before infield warm up started he called me in for a phone call. It was my wife Roni- and she informed me we had a son- Barry William Renna!!

My first at bat I hit a home run!!! When I returned to the bench they gave me the silent treatment- no one said anything to me- no handshakes, pats on the back etc.!! Then all of the sudden they all jumped all over me- & gave me pats on the back etc.

That was quite a thrill- & I have never forgotten it!!

Regards,
Bill Renna

William Beneditto Renna was born in Hanford California in 1924 and played six seasons in the Majors. "Big Bill" played one season for the Yankees; three for the A's and wrapped his career up with the Red Sox. His best season statistically was with the Philadelphia Athletics in 1954 when he hit 13 home runs and plated 53 RBI. As a pinch hitter with Boston in 1958 Renna had 18 RBI on just 15 base hits. During his time he hit 28 four baggers and drove in 119 runs.

Bill Virdon on Bill Mazeroski:

Just being on the 1960 Pirates was a dream come true.

We proved to everyone that we were able to compete with the best team to play the game.

Mazeroski did what we would have all liked to do but when we were-nt the one to do it we were as a whole glad it was him. He was the best 2nd baseman to ever play that position and one of the best people to be associate with.

Sincerely

Bill Virdon

Just being on the 1960 Pirates was a dream come true.

We proved to everyone that we were able to compete with the best team to play the game.

Mazeroski did what we would have all liked to do but when we weren't the one to do it we were as a whole glad it was him. He was the best 2nd baseman to ever play that position and one of the best people to be associated with.

Sincerely,
Bill Virdon

Bill Virdon was named the 1955 National League Rookie of the Year and played 12 seasons in the Big Leagues. Nine of those seasons he started in center field for the Pittsburgh Pirates, including the 1960 World Series Champions. In 1962 Virdon won a National League Gold Glove and led the league in triples with 10. In 5980 at bats he collected 1596 hits good for a .267 average. He also belted 81 triples and 91 home runs. After his playing career Virdon went on to manage 13 seasons in the Majors with four clubs.

His and his teammates' obvious admiration for Bill Mazeroski was well warranted. Mazeroski had his bust unveiled at Cooperstown in 2001.

ON THE MOUND

BUC HILL ACES
KLINE-FRIEND-LAW-FACE

Ned Garver on pitching well for a bad team:

It was very glad to be in the big leagues — glad to be a Brownie — and did not feel sorry for myself.

Ned Garver

Jimmy Bloodworth on Bob Feller:

In 1946 I was Bob Feller's 349th strike out. I never Remember Him allowing me a Hit

Jimmy Bloodworth

Walt Masterson on being appreciated:

BEING SELECTED TO TWO ALL-STAR TEAMS SELECTED TO START THE 1948 GAME IN ST. LOUIS-

SI.

Mel Harder on his career:

Dear Craig:

During my 20 years of pitching for Cleveland, I have had many thrills. I would say, pitching the first game ever played in the new Cleveland Stadium on July 31, 1932 before 80,000 fans. I lost 1-0 to Lefty Grove and the A's, etc.

I also feel proud to have pitched in 4 all-star games and allowing no runs in 13 innings.

Also, being a coach on the 1948 World Champions. Cleveland beat the Boston Braves.

Regards

Mel Harder

Dear Craig,

> *During my 20 years of pitching for Cleveland I had many thrills*

> *I would say pitching the first game ever played in the new Cleveland Stadium on July 31, 1932 before 80,000 fans. I lost 1-0 to Lefty Grove and the Phila. A's.*

> *I also feel proud to have pitched in 4 All Star Games and allowing no runs in 13 innings.*

> *Also, being a coach on the 1948 World Champions. Cleveland beat the Boston Braves.*

> *Regards,*
> *Mel Harder*

Mel Harder pitched 20 seasons in the Majors, all for the Cleveland Indians. He appeared in the All Star Game each year from 1934 through 1937.

In 1934 he led the American League with six complete game shut-outs. Harder had a career record of 223 wins against 186 losses good for a winning percentage of .545. He had two 20 win seasons. In the history of the game only Mel played for 20 years and coached for 20 years. His #18 is retired by Cleveland.

Bill Rogell on great pitching:

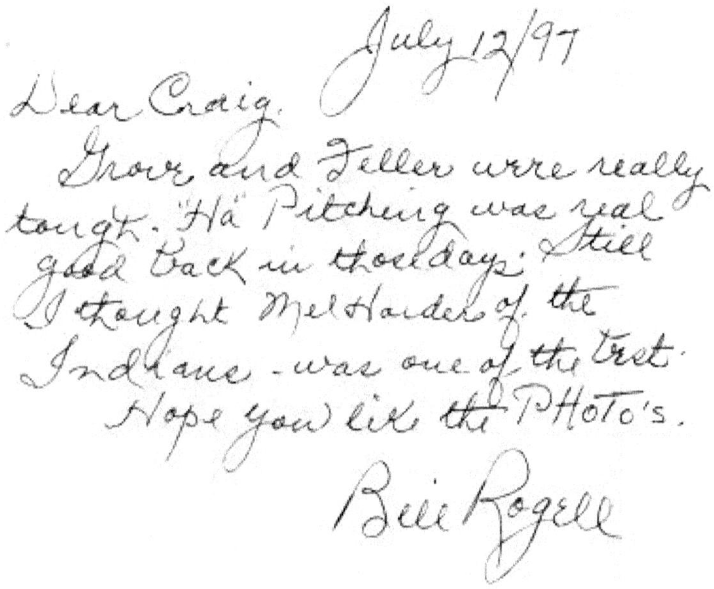

July 12/97

Dear Craig,

Grove and Feller were really tough. "H" Pitching was real good back in those days. Still I thought Mel Harder of the Indians - was one of the best. Hope you lik the PHoTo's.

Bill Rogell

July 12/97

Dear Craig,

Grove and Feller were really tough "Ha". *Pitching was real good back in those days. Still I thought Mel Harder of the Indians was one of the best.*

Hope you like the photos.

Bill Rogell

William George Rogell was born in Springfield Illinois in 1904. He joined the Boston Red Sox in 1925 and spent three seasons there before moving on to Detroit. A durable competitor and fine fielder, Rogell led the American league in games played twice and fielding percentage three times. In 1934 and 1935 he was a member of the American League Pennant winning Detroit Tigers. In '34 the Tigers came up short but in 1935 the World Series title was won by Detroit for the first time in the club's 35 year history.

Harry Danning on catching great games:

There are two games that still happen stick in my memory - both happened in Brooklyn - Carl Hubbell pitched a one hit shut out and pitched to only 27 hitters - a strike out and a throw out at 2nd Base -

The other was Hal Schumacher pitching - the first hitter got a hit and he then picked it to get and the next 27 hitters died in a row

when one was hitting all pitches were too long, but in a slump they were all long -

There are two games that stick in my memory, both happened in Brooklyn. Carl Hubbell pitched a one hit shutout and pitched to only 27 batters, a strike out throw out at second base.

The other was Hal Schumacher pitcher, the first hitter got a hit and he then proceeded it to get out the next 27 in a row.

When we were hitting all the pitchers weren't too tough but when you're in a slump they were all tough.

H.

Harry Danning was born in Los Angeles California in 1911. From 1933 through 1944 "Harry the Horse" was a member of the New York Giants.

From 1937 through 1942 Danning was the starting catcher and was named to four National League All Star Teams appearing in two of the games. He played for the 1936 and 1937 National League Pennant winning New York squads. In both World Series Danning and his mates fell to Gehrig, DiMaggio and the rest of the Bronx Bombers. The 1936 Series went six games and the 1937 went five.

Harry Danning is a member of the Jewish Sports Hall of Fame.

Bob Wolff on calling Larsen's perfect game:

Dear Craig,

In calling this Don Larsen game and becoming increasingly aware of its historical significance, I kept trying not to let the emotion of the game interfere with my play-calling.

I kept giving myself silent "pep talks" to keep describing every action on the field and that's what I did. At game's end, my words "no-hitter", "a perfect game for Don Larsen", "Yogi leaps into Larsen's arms" just poured out.

My body was stiff with tension, my right arm ached — I guess I was pitching the ninth along with Larsen — but it was exhilarating to realize I not only had witnessed a baseball classic but also had broadcast it across the nation and on Armed Forces Network around the world.

Bob Wolff

Dear Craig,

In calling this Don Larsen game and becoming increasingly aware of its historical significance, I kept trying not to let the emotion of the game interfere with my play-calling.

I kept giving myself silent "pep talks" to keep describing every action on the field and that's what I did. At game's end, my words "no-hitter", "a perfect game for Don Larsen", "Yogi leaps into Larsen's arms" just poured out.

My body was stiff with tension, my right arm ached- I guess I was pitching the ninth along with Larsen- but it was exhilarating to realize I not only had witnessed a baseball classic but also had broadcast it across the nation and on Armed Forces Network around the world.

Bob Wolff

Robert Wolff was born in New York City in 1920. He began his broadcasting career in 1939 while enrolled at Duke University. In the history of broadcasting no one has had a longer running continuous career. To this day Wolff can be seen and heard on the Madison Square Garden Network.

Along with Larsen's Perfect Game in the 1956 World Series, Wolff called the 1958 NFL Championship dubbed the "Greatest Game Ever Played", and both of the New York Knicks NBA World Championships.

Bob Wolff was inducted into the Major League Baseball Hall of Fame as the recipient of the Ford C. Frick Award in 1995. There are only two men inducted into both the Baseball and Basketball Halls of Fame; Curt Gowdy and Bob Wolff.

Bob Keegan on his No Hitter:

It was against the ole Washington Senators. Warming up I had my usual stuff fast ball, slider, and change which I never used too much —

Only two or three ball were hit fairly hard and most were ground balls.

It was the biggest thrill of my career and received a check for $1000⁰⁰ from the White Sox. Imagine what I would get now days.

Sincerely
Bob Keegan

BOB KEEGAN PITCHER CHICAGO WHITE SOX

It was against the old Washington Senators. Warming up I had my usual stuff, fast ball, slider and change which I never used too much.

Only two or three balls were hit fairly hard and most were ground balls.

It was the biggest thrill of my career and received a check for $1000.00 from the White Sox. Imagine what I would get now days.

Sincerely,
Bob Keegan

Rochester New York's own Bob Keegan attended Bucknell University before debuting in the Majors as a 32 year old rookie in 1953. He pitched six seasons in the Big Leagues all for the Chicago White Sox.

His finest year was 1954 when he won 16 games and was named to the All Star Team. Keegan pitched in 135 games winning 40 and losing 36. He had 29 complete games including six complete game shut outs.

Keegan's no-hitter came in the second game of a double header at old Comisky Park.

Rich Billings on catching Jim Bibby's No Hitter:

Catching Jim Bibby's no-hitter against the Oakland A's was one of my biggest thrills in the major leagues. I didn't think much about it until around the 7th inning & the pressure began to mount. I remember that Sal Bando hit a towering pop fly between home & third & I started calling for the 3rd baseman to catch it. I wanted no part of spoiling the no-hitter. The 3rd baseman caught it 2 steps from home plate!

Thanks for your letter,

Rich Billings

Catching Jim Bibby's no-hitter against the Oakland A's was one of my biggest thrills in the Major Leagues. I didn't think much about it until around the 7th inning & the pressure began to mount. I remember that Sal Bando hit a towering pop fly between home & third & I started calling for the 3rd baseman to catch it. I wanted no part of spoiling the no-hitter. The 3rd baseman caught it 2 steps from home plate!

Thanks for your letter,
Rich Billings

Richard Arlin Billings began his life in Detroit Michigan in 1942. He began his Major League career with the Washington Senators in 1968. Billings spent six seasons as a backstop in the Big Leagues. He accompanied the Senators to Texas as they became the Rangers. 1972 marked the first year of existence of the Rangers and Billings' finest season. That year he hit safely 119 times for a .254 average while plating 58 runs. 1972 was his best offensive season which corresponded with the most appearances of his career with 133.

Buddy Lewis on Bob Feller:

Bob Feller: (before WW2 - /eave)

Feller was very fast -- hard for me to foul-a-ball prior to one entry into WWII. -- His fast pitch would rise so suddenly that I laid off of any thing above the waist -- which made him develop a curve (overhand) breaking down -- This did me in!!

After WWII, he had lost this advantage --

Bud

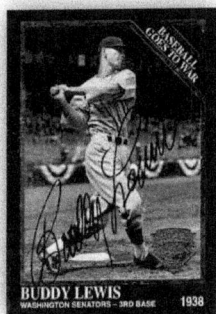

Bob Feller: (before WW2-leave)

> *Feller was very fast hard for me to foul-a-ball prior to our entry into WWII. His fast pitch would rise so suddenly that I laid off of anything above the waist- which made him develop a curve (overhand) breaking down- This did me in!!*
>
> *After WWII, he had lost this advantage.*
>
> *BL*

John Kelly "Buddy" Lewis was born in Gastonia North Carolina in 1916. Beginning in 1935 he spent eleven seasons in the Major Leagues all with the Washington Senators.

In the field Lewis played the hot corner for his first five seasons and the outfield for the rest of his career. It was with a bat in his hands that he really showed his prowess. With his 5261 plate appearances Lewis had 1563 hits, accounting for his .297 clip. In 1939 he led the American League with 16 triples that contributed to the 93 he hit for his tenure. He also belted 71 round trippers and 249 doubles.

Lewis was named to and played in two All Star Games. His appearances in the mid summer classics were separated by several years, 1938 and 1947.

Virgil Trucks on his career:

Hi Craig,
Just a few lines in answer to your question. The very first thrill of my career was my first year in baseball which was Class D in the minor leagues. It would be classified today as A or AA. I won 26 lost 6 - ERA of 1.25 pitched 2 no hitters in 1938 in the Alabama-Fl league. Struckout 450 batters. 420 in the regular season & 30 in the play-offs. And of course my greatest thrill or should I say thrills. Was to play in the major leagues - 2 all star games, winning one & saving the other. 1 world series win. And the best of all is stamped below. Also enclosed is a Print of me & my major league stats. Good luck in your collection.

Sincerely,
Virgil "Fire" Trucks

2-No hitters-1952
Washington-R.H.E.
0.0.0.-5-15-52
New York-R.H.E.
0.0.0.-8-25-52

Hi Craig,

Just a few lines in answer to your question The very first thrill of my career was my first year in baseball which was Class D in the minor leagues. It would be classified today as A or AA. I won 26 lost 6- ERA of 1.25, pitched 2 no hitters in 1938 in the Alabama Fall Fl League. Struck out 450 batters, 420 in the regular season & 30 in the play offs. And of course my greatest thrill or should I say thrills was to play in the Major Leagues- 2 All Star Games winning one & saving the other. One a World Series win and the best of all is stamped below. Also enclosed is a print of me & my Major League stats. Good luck in your collection.

> *Sincerely*
> *Virgil "Fire" Trucks*

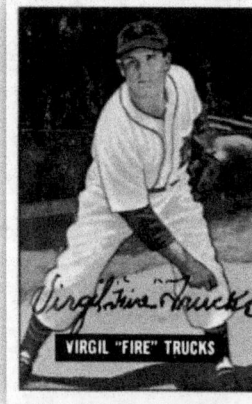

Virgil Trucks pitched 17 seasons in the Big Leagues for six clubs. In his two All Star seasons he led the league in complete game shut outs. In 1949 Trucks led the league in strike outs with 153. His career mark of 177 wins to 135 losses good for a .567 winning percentage. He struck out 1534 batters in 2682.1 innings of work. Virgil Trucks is the great-uncle of the talented and successful blues guitarist Derek Trucks.

Ace Adams on his biggest thrills:

Dear Brag:

My biggest thrill was pitching against Brooklyn opening day 1941 and winning which was the first Major League game I had ever seen.

I had many more thrills throughout my career, broke several records relieving, set 70 games in 1943

Please excuse my writing I hurt my good hand

Cordially
Ace Adams
N.Y. Giants
1941—1946

Dear Craig,

My biggest thrill was pitching against Brooklyn opening day 1941 and winning which was the first major league game I had ever seen.

I had many more thrills throughout my career. Broke several records relieving, pit[ched] 70 games in 1943.

Please excuse my writing I hurt my good hand.

Sincerely
Ace Adams
N. Y. Giants
1941-1946

Ace Adams (Ace was his given name) was born in Willows, California in 1912. He pitched six seasons in the Majors all for the New York Giants. Used almost exclusively as a relief pitcher throughout his career (he made 7 career starts), Adams led the National League in appearances in 1942, '43 and '44. He also topped the National League in saves in 1944 and '45 with 13 and 15 respectively. In 1943 he was named to the National League All Star team. Adams had 302 appearances in his six seasons averaging 50 a season, a staggering amount of relief work at the time. In 302 appearances Ace amassed a record of 41 wins versus 33 losses and also tallied 49 saves.

Bob Kuzava on World Series saves:

Clay

I was in three Series, and it was a real nice feeling. We had some great players. The period as you know, was in the 1950's I was lucky enough to save the 51 and 52 last games, and I guess that was my biggest three. I guess that record still stands, two saves in two years.

Again, thanks for your interest and nice letter. Wish you and your's the best.

Yours in baseball
Bob

Craig,

I was in the Series, and it was a real nice feeling We had some great players.

The period as you know, was in the 1950s. I was lucky enough to save the '51 and '52 last games and I guess that record still stands. Two saves in two years.

Again thanks for your interest and nice letter. Wish you and yours the best.

Yours in baseball
Bob

Bob Kuzava pitched ten seasons in the Major Leagues for seven teams. Though used mainly as a reliever throughout his career, he had 34 complete games including seven complete game shut outs.

Kuzava had a career record of 49 wins against 44 losses. He also amassed 13 regular season saves to go with his World Series saves.

Tot Pressnell on his career:

I am 92 yrs old, can't write to good.
In 38 I went to the ~~Dodgers~~. My first game was a
shut out 6 to 0. I pitched against Van Lingle in his
2 no hitter. Was put on the 1938 rookie team.
In 39 I pitch the first televised game Bet Cinn. 4-2
Had some good year in Milwakee. In 36 I won 23
games In 37 - 19 - In 34 16.

Your friend
Tot Pressnell

I am 92 years old, can't write too good.

In '38 I went to the Dodgers. My first game was a shut out 6 to 0, I pitched against Vander Meer in his 2nd no hitter. Was put on the 1938 rookie team.

In '39 I pitched the first televised game. Beat Cinci[nnati] 4-2.

Had some good years in Milwaukee. In '36 I won 23 games. In '37- 19 in '34- 16.

Your friend,
Tot Pressnell

Forest Charles Pressnell was born in 1906 in Findlay, OH. It was not until 1938 that he broke into the Major Leagues with the Brooklyn Dodgers. His rookie season he pitched in 43 games, starting 19. Of those 43 appearances Pressnell won 11 games and saved three in relief.

In his three seasons and 98 appearances with the Dodgers "Tot" won 26 games including four complete game shut-outs. He also notched 7 saves. From Brooklyn Pressnell moved on to the Chicago Cubs of the National League. In two seasons with the Cubs Pressnell earned six wins and five saves.

In five Big League seasons Pressnell competed in 154 contests. He had a 32 and 30 record with 17 complete games including four complete game shut-outs.

Bill Monbouquette on his No-Hitter:

Craig,
It was the most exciting moment of my career. What a feeling. They say I jumped about five feet off the ground. I hadn't won a game for I guess around a month. Flying in from Boston that day the stewardess sat down next to me as I was doing a crossword puzzle and asked how I was doing. I said oh I've been struggling of late, and turned and said, oh well you'll pitch a no hitter tonight and I guess you could say thats was history.
All the best
Bill Monbouquette

Craig,

     It was the most exciting moment of my career. What a feeling. They say I jumped about five feet off the ground. I hadn't won a game for I guess around a month. Flying in from Boston that day the stewardess sat down next to me as I was doing a crossword puzzle and asked how I was doing. I said "Oh I've been struggling of late", and [she] turned and said "Oh well, you'll pitch a no hitter tonight". And I guess you could say that was history.

     All the Best,
     Bill Monbouquette

     Bill Monbouquette pitched 11 seasons in the Major Leagues. He was named to three All-Star teams, pitching in one of the games. In a 1961 game against the Washington Senators Monbouquette set a Red Sox team record with 17 strike outs. His best season was 1963 when he won 20 games against 10 losses. Overall he won 114 games including his no-hitter. Bill was inducted into the Red Sox Hall of Fame in 2000.

George Zuverink on his 11 inning shut out:

Because the 4th of July was on Sunday in 1954 we celebrated the double hear on July the 5th.

I was scheduled to pitch the 2nd game so I had to sit & watch the first game when Cleveland beat the Tigers 16-5. Boy was that tough to watch from the dugout and then I'd go to the locker room.

Anyway I did get to pitch the 2nd game – We won 1 to 0 in 11 innings, Harvey Kuenn hit a home in the bottom of the 11th, WE WON! What a thrill as I pitched a 3 hitter. A lot of my friends from my home town of Holland, Mich were at the game.

George Zuverink

TIGERS' BIG BATS
HARVEY KUENN • AL KALINE

Because the 4th of July was on Sunday in 1954 we celebrated the double header on Monday the 5th.

I was scheduled to pitch the 2nd game so I had to sit and watch the first game when Cleveland beat the Tigers 16-5. Boy was that tough to watch from the dugout and then I'd go to the locker room.

Anyway I did get to pitch the 2nd game. We won 1 to 0 in 11 innings. Harvey Kuenn hit a home run in the bottom of the 11th, WE WON! What a thrill as I pitched a 3 hitter. A lot of my friends from my home town of Holland, Mich. were at the game.

George Zuverink

With the last name Zuverink, George's is the last name listed among Major League pitchers ever to have taken the mound. However, George would go on to finish first in categories that were not alphabetical.

In 1924 Holland Michigan welcomed George Zuverink. 27 years later the Major Leagues followed suit. He bounced around the systems of the Cleveland Indians, the Cincinnati Reds and the Detroit Tigers before landing with the Baltimore Orioles half way through the 1955 season.

By 1956 Zuverink was one of the premier relievers in the American League. He led the League in saves and appearances that year with 16 and 62 respectively. In 1957 he appeared in 56 games to again top the circuit.

Hugh Mulcahy on his first appearance:

Hi Craig,

1/21/99

Happy to answer your letter

My greatest thrill was when I first pitched in the Major League. It was July, 1935 in Forbes Field, Pitts., Pa., home of the Pitt. Pirates. I had to relieve one inning and the three batters I had to face were Paul Waner, Lloyd Waner and 'Arky' Vaughn. I was lucky and retired all three.

Perhaps my next greatest thrill was when I was named on the 1940 National League All-Star team although I didn't get to pitch.

Best wishes,

Hugh Mulcahy

11/21/99

Hi Craig,

Happy to answer your letter.

My greatest thrill was when I first pitched in the Major Leagues. It was July, 1935 in Forbes Field, Pitts., PA home of the Pitts. 'Pirates'. I had to relieve one inning and the three batters I had to face were Paul Waner, Lloyd Waner and 'Arky' Vaughn. I was lucky and retired all three.

Perhaps my next greatest thrill was when I was named on the 1941 National League All Star Team although I didn't get to pitch.

Best Wishes,
Hugh Mulcahy

Hugh Mulcahy pitched nine seasons in the Major Leagues. Eight of those seasons were spent with the Philadelphia Phillies along with a two appearance stint with the Pittsburgh Pirates to wind up his career in 1947. He was used as both a starting pitcher and a reliever during his tenure. His 56 appearances led the National League in 1937.

Hugh was nicknamed "Losing Pitcher" Mulcahy as he pitched well for some very poor teams. Throughout his time with the Phillies, his teams finished out of last place only once. Proof of this is the 1941 season that he was named to the All Star Team. That year his record was 13 wins against 22 losses.

Mulcahy was the very first of many Major Leaguers drafted into the Armed Services for World War II. If Mulcahy ever lived up to his nick name it was in 1944. That year Danny Litwhiler hit a homer to win the World Series for the Phillies. While he was serving his country Hugh Mulcahy lost his opportunity to finally pitch for a winner.

THE WORLD SERIES

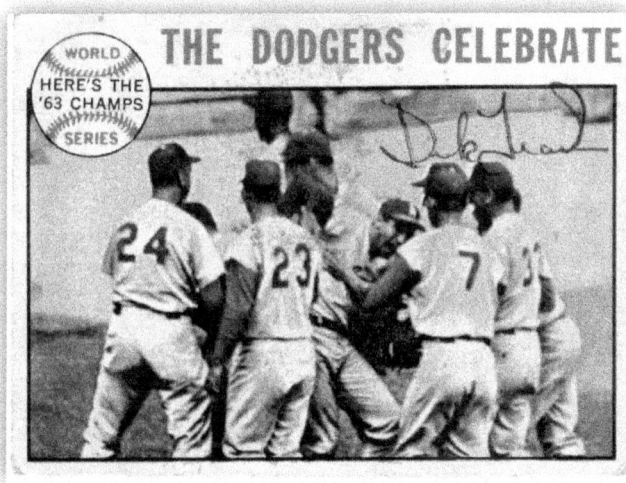

Whitey Kurowski on his homer in the 1942 Series:

> It was a great thrill to hit the home run
> to help win the game we had a great team
>
> Best wishes
> Whitey Kurowski

Al Gionfriddo on his greatest thrill in the Majors:

> I had many thrill in baseball
> and making the catch in the
> 1947 world series was one
> of the biggest.
>
> AL

Elroy Face on his greatest thrill:

> My greatest thrill, was winning
> the World Series, against the
> New York Yankees.
>
> Elroy Face

Tony Kubek on the World Series:

My biggest personal world series thrill came during my rookie year, 1957. I was fortunate (Lucky) to hit two HRs in game no. 3, the first WS game ever played in Milwaukee. I was born and raised in Milwaukee. Unfortunately, we lost that series in 7 games.

My biggest team thrill and I think a more important one came in 1958 when we beat the Milwaukee Braves for the world championship.

Regards,
Tony Kubek

TONY KUBEK
SHORTSTOP

My biggest personal World Series thrill came during my rookie year, 1957. I was fortunate (lucky) to hit two HRs in game no. 3 the first W.S. game ever played in Milwaukee. I was born and raised in Milwaukee. Unfortunately, we lost that series in 7 games.

My biggest team thrill and I think a more important one came in 1958 when we beat the Milwaukee Braves for the World Championship.

Regards,
Tony Kubek

Tony Kubek was born in Milwaukee Wisconsin in 1936. He debuted with the New York Yankees in 1957 and went on to be named the American League Rookie of the Year. Kubek went on to be named to three American League All Star teams playing in two of the events. He was also a member of three World Series Championship clubs.

After his playing career Kubek went on to as a television commentator. He worked a myriad of big games. One of the biggest was as the third man in the booth for Hank Aaron's record breaking 715th home run. Always outspoken, Kubek derided National League President Bowie Kuhn on the air for not attending the game. Kuhn responded by saying he had an engagement that could not be broken.

In 2009 Tony Kubek was inducted into Cooperstown and the recipient of the Ford Frick Award for broadcasting. Kubek was the first person to receive the Frick as strictly a television broadcaster.

Jim Kaat on the World Series:

Pitching in the 1965 World Series
against Sandy Koufax was great
but what topped them all was
being a member of the 1982
World champion St. Louis Cardinals!

Best Regards,
Jim Kaat

JIM KAAT
PITCHER

Pitching in the 1965 World Series against Sandy Koufax was great but what topped them all was being a member of the 1982 World Champion St. Louis Cardinals!

Best Regards
Jim Kaat

Jim Kaat pitched 25 seasons in the Major Leagues third most in history behind Nolan Ryan and Tommy John. During his quarter of a century in the bigs, Kaat won 283 games against 237 losses. An excellent athlete, he won 16 Gold Gloves for fielding his position which was a record that stood until Greg Maddux won his 17th and 18th. Further proving his athleticism Kaat hit 16 home runs and often batted in the eighth spot in the lineup. A pitcher batting ahead of a position player in a lineup has been basically unheard of since.

He was named to three American League All Star games pitching in two of them. Kaat had three 20 win seasons including a league leading total of 25 in 1966.

After his playing days Kaat went in to broadcasting and has won 7 Emmys for his work as a color commentator.

Johnny Hopp on the World Series:

Playing in my first
World Series is my biggest thrill-
1942, as a Cardinal player we
defeated a great yankee team)
4 games to 1 in 1943, They won
the first game in St Louis, we
won the 3 rd, and then on to
yankee Stadium where we won
3 straight. I played in total of
5 world series, 4 winners
and 1 loser

Good luck with
your hobby
Johnny Hopp

Playing in my first World Series is my biggest thrill- 1942 as a Cardinal player we defeated the great Yankee team 4 games to 1 in 1942. They won the first game in St. Louis we won the 2nd, and then on to Yankee Stadium where we won 3 straight. I played in total of 5 World Series, 4 winners and 1 loser.

Good luck with your hobby
Johnny Hopp

John Leonard Hopp was born in Hastings Nebraska in 1916. He played outfield and 1rst base for six teams over his 14 season career.

In 1946 Hopp was named to the National League All Star squad as a member of the Boston Braves. In 1393 games Hopp collected 1262 hits in 4260 plate appearances good for a .296 career average.

He belted 216 doubles, 74 triples and 46 home runs.

Danny Litwhiler on his biggest baseball thrills:

Playing my first major league game in 1940 for the Philadelphia Phillies and hitting a home run in a World Series game to win the game 2-0, thus helping to win the World Championships in 1944.

Danny Litwhiler

Playing my first Major League game in 1940 for the Philadelphia Phillies and hitting a home run in the World Series game to win the game 2-0, thus helping to win the World Championship in 1944.

Danny Litwhiler

Daniel Webster Litwhiler was born in 1916 in Ringtown PA. In his third season in the Majors he was named to the National League All Star team. After joining the St. Louis Cardinals Litwhiler participated in two World Series. He went on to play with Boston Braves and wound up his 11 year career with the Cincinnati Reds in 1951.

After his playing career Litwhiler went into coaching. From 1955 through 1963 he skippered the Florida State University squad to a 189 win and 81 loss record and three College World Series appearances.

In 1964 he moved on to Michigan State University. Litwhiler coached the Spartans through 1982 leading them to a 488 and 363 record. During his tenure he produced several quality players that went on to productive professional careers including Rich Billings, Steve Garvey and Kirk Gibson.

Danny Litwhiler's quality instruction of college ballplayers led to his induction into the Baseball Coaches Hall of Fame.

Frank Mancuso on the World Series:

Dear Craig:

Sorry your letter got misplaced. There is no feeling like playing in a world series.

I'm sure any major leaguer will say that. Many play their whole career and never have the experience. I was young and the year before was in the service (paratroops).

The season itself was tough. We won the pennant on the last day.

Just playing against great players like Musial, Cooper Brothers, Marty Marion and all the Cardinals was a thrill.

We had a chance to win it all but didn't get the breaks.

About all I can say Craig is it was the biggest thrill a baseball player can have.

Thanks
Frank Mancuso

Dear Craig;

> *Sorry your letter got misplaced.*
> *There is no feeling like playing in a World Series.*
> *I'm sure any Major Leaguer will say that.*
> *Many play their whole career and never have the experience.*
> *I was young and the year before was in the service. (para troopers)*
> *The season itself was tough. We won the pennant on the last day.*
> *Just playing against great players like Musial, Cooper Brothers, Marty Marion and all the Cardinals was a great thrill.*
> *We had a chance to win it all but didn't get the breaks.*
> *About all I can say Craig is it was the biggest thrill a baseball player can have.*

> *Thanks,*
> *Frank Mancuso*

Frank Mancuso caught Major League pitching for four seasons starting in 1944. He played three seasons for the St. Louis Browns and one for the Washington Senators. Frank's brother Gus was also a catcher and played 17 seasons in the Majors. The brothers Mancuso combined for 1797 career games caught.

Bobby Brown on the World Series:

In the seventh game of the 1947 World Series (Yankees - Dodgers) I was put in to pinch hit in the middle of the game. The Yankees were behind 2 to 1 with two men on base. I hit a two base hit that tied up the game at 2 to 2 with runners remaining on third and second. The go ahead run was scored, and the Yankees went on to win the game and the Series. When I hit the double that tied the game, and stood on second base listening to the roar of the crowd. That was my biggest thrill

Bobby Brown

In the seventh game of the 1947 World Series (Yankees-Dodgers) I was put in to pinch hit in the middle of the game. The Yankees were behind 2 to 1 with two men on base. I hit a two base hit that tied up the game at 2 to 2 with runners remaining on third and second. The go ahead run was scored and the Yankees went on to win the game and the Series. When I hit the double that tied the game and stood on second base listening to the roar of the crowd that was my biggest thrill.

Bobby Brown

Robert William Brown played 3rd base for eight seasons in the Major Leagues all with the New York Yankees. He played the "hot corner" for four World Series winning Bronx Bomber squads. Brown played 548 games for the Yankees and batted .279 for his career.

30 years after his playing days Brown went on to be the President of the American League for ten years from 1984 through 1994. On Rawling's Official American League baseballs during that period, Bobby Brown's facsimile autograph can be found on the sweet spot. The end of his tenure in that capacity was brought about by the National and American League President positions being absorbed by the commissioner's office.

Jimmy Outlaw on Game 7:

Eversince I was a little boy I went to play big league base ball. I always dreamed of playing in the big leagues I didn't play ball in high school but after finishing school I was just three years in pro ball. Finally I was playing with Detroit Tigers from '43 - '45. We were in the World Series in 1945, we playing the Chicago Cubs. The series went 7 game and we won the seventh game. When I caught the ball for the out that ended the 7th game and win, was the biggest thrill of my career.

Jimmy Outlaw

Ever since I was a little boy I wanted to play baseball. I always dreamed of playing in the big leagues. I didn't play ball in high school but after finishing school I was just three years in pro ball. Finally I was playing with Detroit Tigers from '43-'45. We won in the World Series in 1945. We played the Chicago Cubs. The series went 7 games and we won the seventh game. When I caught the ball for the out that ended the 7th game and win was the biggest thrill of my career.

Jimmy Outlaw

Jimmy Outlaw started his decade long Big League career with a two year stint beginning in 1937 as a 3rd baseman for the Cincinnati Reds. In 1939 he spent 65 games with the Boston Braves of the National League before going on to his greatest success with the Detroit Tigers.

Outlaw moved from 3rd base to the outfield upon joining the Tigers. Showing that strong 3rd baseman's arm in 1944 he led all American League outfielders with 14 assists. In the 1945 World Series Outlaw shifted back to the hot corner for all seven games of the series. During his decade long career Outlaw batted .268 and had a fielding percentage of .972.

Lennie Merullo on the 1945 World Series:

Craig,

Your note has finally caught up to me here in Ft Myers Florida where I'm covering college on their Spring trip. Will head back to New England this weekend.

You asked about my experience of playing in '45 World Series.

Naturally it was very exciting — All the fan fare etc. I only played in two of the games however and that was a disappointment along to losing the Tigers in 7 games.

I am still in baseball and like you enjoying it very much just watching young players develop.

Again thanks for making this ol' timers feel good!

Good luck
Lennie Merullo

Craig,

Your note has finally caught up to me here in Ft. Myers Florida where I'm covering colleges on their spring trip. Will head back to New England this weekend.

You asked about my experience of playing in '45 World Series.

Naturally it was very exciting- all the fan fare etc. I only played in two of the games however and that was a disappointment along to losing to (the) Tigers in 7 games.

I am still in baseball and like you enjoying it very much just watching young players develop.

Again thanks for making this ol' timer feel good!!

Good Luck
Lennie Merullo

Lennie Merullo
Diamond Greats # 107

Life-time	G	H	2B	R	RBI	BA
	639	497	92	191	152	.240

Lenny Merullo played short stop for the Cincinnati Reds for seven seasons. In 639 games Merullo collected 497 hits including 92 doubles.

His grandson Matt played catcher for six seasons in the Big Leagues.

Joe Moore on winning the World Series:

you Know every One Loves a Winner and I must
say with out a daubt that winning a World
Series would gelladifi as almost a Miracle
you can't beat a Winner
                              Joe Moore
                              NY Giants 1930-1941

"JO-JO" MOORE

You know everyone loves a winner and I must say without a doubt that winning a World Series would qualify as almost a miracle. You can't beat a winner.

Joe Moore
NY Giants 1930-1941

Joseph Gregg "Jo Jo" Moore was born in 1908 in Gause, Texas. "The Gause Ghost" roamed the outfield for a dozen seasons for the New York Giants.

In 1932 Moore had a 20 game hit streak in the regular season. In 1335 games all for the Giants, he batted .298 and plated 513 runs. While known as a free swinger Moore had an acute batting eye. In 5427 career plate appearances he struck out a mere 247 times. The 247 lifetime K's translates to 4.6% of his career at bats that he was sent back to the dugout without making contact with strike three.

In 1933, 1936 and 1937 Moore participated in the World Series. In 1933 The New York Giants won the World Series, in '36 and '37 they took the National League pennant and fell to the Yankees in the Series. In the '37 Series Moore tied a record by recording nine hits in a five game series.

Named to six National League All Star squads, Moore appeared in four of the contests.

HISTORY

John Babich on his favorite player growing up:

> Babe Ruth was my favorite, I guess all young Players felt the same
>
> *John Babich*

Billy Pierce on playing for Hall Of Fame manager Connie Mack:

> For a 17 year old it was quite a thrill.
>
> *Bill Pierce*

Ray Boone on his favorite player growing up:

> My FAVORITE PLAYER WAS BIG HANK GREENBERG 1B FOR DETROIT TIGERS. HALL of FAMER.
>
> *Ray Boone*

Bobby Bragan on Branch Rickey:

Dear Craig,

My biggest thrill in baseball was getting to know and to respect and to love Mr. Branch Rickey.

He was the greatest person to ever walk on the sports stage. So many innovations and so much influence on the game and those of us in it.

He broke the color line with Jackie Robinson. He founded Dodgertown at Vero Beach, Fla- We were the first to have a complex- 4 fields etc. Now all clubs have them. He and Norman Vincent Peale founded the Fellowship of Christian Athletes. He invented the baseball helmet in the basement of Forbes Field, Pittsburgh, PA.

He established the Gas House Gang at St. Louis where speed was emphasized. He was the first person to put special emphasis on speed for he knew that it was effective on offense and defense.

He caused expansion of the Major Leagues by attempting to form a 3rd Major League.

I'm sure I speak for many, many people; Walter Alston, Tom Lasorda, Stan the Man, Red Schoendienst, Buzzie Bavasi, Gabe Paul and hundreds of executives and field personnel.

Hope this helps you somehow.

Sincerely,
Bobby Bragan

Bobby Bragan played seven seasons in the Majors with the Philadelphia Phillies and the Brooklyn Dodgers. He played short stop, catcher and 3rd base. Bragan was a member of the Dodgers team that participated in the first televised World Series, a seven game loss to the New York Yankees.

Crash Davis on being Crash Davis:

Craig, my greatest thrill was the day I reported to the Phila A's - The gateman knew my name!! My dream had come true, "I was in the Big League"!!

To be a part of "Bull Durham" has simply been Amazing - I've had so much fun being "Crash Davis"

Crash

Craig, my greatest thrill was the day I reported to the Phila A's. The gateman knew my name!! My dream had come true, "I was in the Big Leagues"!!

To be a part of "Bull Durham" has simply been amazing. I've had so much fun being "Crash Davis".

Crash

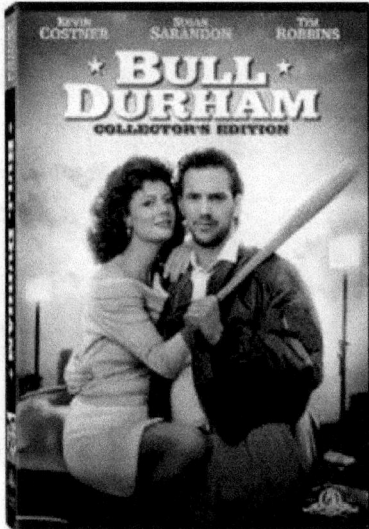

Lawrence Columbus Davis was born in Canon Georgia in 1919. "Crash" played 2nd base in 148 games over three seasons for Connie Mack's Philadelphia Athletics. He hit for a .230 average with 2 home runs and 43 RBIs in his Major League career.

His minor league baseball career was a basis for Kevin Costner's character in the classic baseball movie "Bull Durham."

Tom Saffell on Honus Wagner:

Dear Craig,

Mr Wagner was a very nice man but in 1951 when I was Pittsburg he did not dress out. He sat in the R.F. tunnel in a chair just at the opening of the tunnel so he could watch the ball game. He gave some advice to our short stop (Stan Rojek) but he did not come out on the field — he must have been about 80 years old at that time. I did get autograph on a ball. In 1917 he was mgr + player. His last active year.

Tom Saffell

Dear Craig,

  Mr. Wagner was a very nice man but in 1951 when I was with Pittsburgh, he did not dress out. He sat in the R.F. (right field) tunnel in a chair just at the opening of the tunnel so he could watch the ball game. He gave some advice to our short stop (Stan Rojek) but he did not come out on the field- he must have been about 80 years old at that time. I did get an autograph on a ball. In 1917 he was mgr & player. His last active year.

  Tom Saffell

Thomas Saffell was born in Etowah, Tennessee in 1921. He debuted with the Pirates in 1949 and played through the 1951 season. After a four year stint as a Navy pilot, Saffell had a brief Major League swan song splitting the 1955 season with the Pirates and the A's.

After his Big League career Tom went on to manage several minor league teams. In his first season as manager he led the Reno Silver Sox to a California League title in 1960 and later took the Midwest League crown in 1969 as skipper of the Appleton Foxes. His minor league managerial tenure lasted a dozen seasons. In 1980 Saffell took over as President of the Gulf Coast League. He held that position for nearly three decades before retiring in 2009 at the age of 88.

The legend of the Honus Wagner T206 tobacco card is fairly well known. Wagner was one of the nation's biggest celebrities during his playing days and endorsed products much like prominent athletes do today. However Wagner was concerned with children smoking tobacco and demanded that his image be removed from the card set soon after its production. Because of this the T206 Wagner card is by far the most rare and valuable baseball card ever issued and when one of the few copies changes hands it usually brings hundreds of thousands dollars in return.

Hal Trosky Jr. on his Father and today's Pro:

Hi Craig:

Quite frankly, Craig, my Father's Major League career had absolutely no effect on me during the years that I played baseball.

My Father commanded the utmost respect of his peers in both the AL + NL. He was a man of great humility, team oriented to the NTH degree, thus was team Captain for the Indians for several years.

If there is one single thing that had a parallel with the players of his era, and my era, was that the "Fans were King"!! The money the fans paid for tickets was the source of our paycheck. Since the 70's, the revenue paid for the ludicrous salaries of players today, thus, the players have little or no contact with the fans. It makes me sick to see the after effects. There is not a single Professional Athlete, in any sport, that is "WORTH" anymore than 1/5th of what they are being paid!!!

My apologies for going on a tangent that really didn't address your question, Craig, but I feel very deeply about what I'd addressed.

I'm extremely proud of playing during the times when the "FAN WAS KING To EVERY PRO ATHLETE"!! ..... my most treasured memory while playing the game!!!!

Best regards,

Hal Trosky, Jr.

Hi Craig:

Quite frankly, Craig, my father's Major League career had absolutely no effect on me during the years that I played pro ball.

My father commanded the utmost respect of his peers in both the AL & NL. He was a man of great humility, team oriented to the Nth degree, thus was team captain for the Indians for several years.

If there is one single thing that had a parallel with the players of his era and my era was the "Fans Were King!!". The money the fans paid for tickets was the source of our paycheck. Since the 70's, TV revenue paid the ludicrous salaries of players today, thus, the players have little or no contact with the fans. It makes me sick to see the after effects. There is not a single Professional Athlete in any sport that is "WORTH" any more than 1/5 of what they are being paid!!!

My apologies for going on a tangent that really didn't address your question, Craig. But I feel very deeply about what I've expressed.

I'm extremely proud of playing during the times when "FAN WAS KING TO EVERY PRO ATHLETE!!!!"... My most treasured memory while playing the game!!!!

Best regards,
Hal Trosky Jr.

Harold Arthur Trosky Jr. was born in Cleveland OH in 1936. His Big League career consisted of three relief innings pitched over two games for the Chicago White Sox in 1958. For his brief five inning of work he earned a strike out, a win and a perfect won/lost record.

The elder Hal Trosky spent eleven years in the Major Leagues all with the Cleveland Indians. He played first base for the Tribe from 1933 to 1946. During his tenure he belted 228 homers including a career best 42 in 1936, the year his son was born.

Eddie Collins Jr. on being a Hall of Famer's son:

Dear Craig,

There really wasn't any problem. My father retired in 1930 and I broke in in '39 so there were many players still active who knew him or knew a lot about him and he was highly respected. Among the players I very often felt that many of them were pulling for me to do well — out of admiration & respect for my father.

Among the fans it was different. All players get yelled at and in my case it simply determined what they would yell, not why. "You aren't as good as your old man" — that sort of thing. By reacting with a smile and not being adversarial they would usually mellow and I got along ok with the bleacherites.

Eddie Collins

Dear Craig,
      There really wasn't any problem. My father retired in 1930 and I broke in in '39 so there were many players still around who knew him or knew a lot about him and he was highly respected. Among the players I very often felt that many of them were pulling for me to do well out of admiration and respect for my father.

      Among the fans it was different. All players get yelled at and in my case it simply determined what they would yell not why. "You aren't as good as your old man", that sort of thing. By returning with a smile and not being adversarial they would usually mellow and I got along ok with the bleacherites.

   Eddie Collins

      Edward Trowbridge Collins Jr. was born in Landsdowne Pennsylvania in 1916 and went on to play 3 seasons with the Philadelphia Athletics. He had a .241 batting average in 274 plate appearances.

      His father Eddie Collins Sr. played 25 seasons in the Major Leagues. He was a member of the 1919 "Black Sox" although he was not involved in the fix of the World Series. Eddie Sr. was inducted into the Hall of Fame in 1939, the same year his son made his Major League debut.

Cecil Travis on Satchel Paige:

In Regard to Satchel Paige — The only
time I played against Satchel was
2 Exhibition games in 1942 at Chicago
& Washington   Dizzy Dean allstars vs. Satchel Paige All Stars
while I was in Military Service —
He was treated great by the Fans
& players —

Cecil H. Travis

In regards to Satchel Paige- The only time I played against Satchel was 2 exhibition games in 1942 at Chicago and Washington. Dizzy Dean All Stars vs. Satchel Paige All Stars.
He was treated great by the fans and the players.

Cecil H. Travis

Cecil Travis was a Big Leaguer for 12 seasons all with the Washington Senators. It is widely believed that Travis would have had Hall of Fame statistics had his prime not been lost to service in World War II. He was named to three American League All Star teams and played in two of the games.

Travis had a lifetime batting average of .314. In 1941, the year before he entered the service, he had his finest season. That year he led the American League in hits with 218 while batting at a .359 clip. That .359 average was good for a distant second place in the American League behind Ted Williams' .406.

Travis played for three seasons after he returned from his four year stint the armed forces. The time away had obviously affected his skill on the diamond. He failed to hit .260 after having batted .300 or better in eight of his previous nine pre-war seasons.

Eddie Joost on Connie Mack:

The years I spent with Mr. Mack
and the Phila. A's, were the best years
of my baseball life.
- Mr. Mack was a grand Old Man
Eddie Joost

The years I spent with Mr. Mack and the Phila. A's were the best years of my baseball life.

Mr. Mack was a grand Old Man

Eddie Joost

Edwin David Joost was born in San Francisco CA in 1916. Two Decades later he began his Major League career with the Cincinnati Red Legs. In 1940 Joost was a member of the World Series winning Reds.

After a brief two season stint with Boston, Joost had a successful eight season stint with the Philadelphia A's. During this period he was named to two American League All Star squads.

Over his 17 seasons in the Big Leagues, Eddie Joost played the infield for four clubs. He participated in 1574 games, amassing 1339 hits 134 of which were round trippers.

Cornelius Alexander McGillicuddy was born in 1862 in East Brookfield, MA. He shortened his name to Connie Mack and played catcher in the Majors for 11 seasons. During the final three seasons of his playing career Mack was a player/manager for the Pittsburgh Pirates.

Beginning in 1901 Mack managed the Philadelphia Athletics for 49 years winning five World Series. To this day his all time records for most wins and most losses stand. In 1937 Connie Mack was inducted into the Baseball Hall Of Fame in Cooperstown. He was the last manager to wear street clothes in the dugout.

George Kell on career thrills:

I thank being Elected to the Hall of Fame was my greatest thrill. Winning the batting Title in the 1949 Season was very pleasing - but there were many more in a Fifteen year Career -

Sincerely
George Kell
Hof 83

I think being elected to the Hall of Fame was the greatest thrill. Winning the batting title in 1949 season was very pleasing, but there were many more in a fifteen year career.

Sincerely,
George Kell
HOF '83

Swifton, Arkansas' own George Kell was a 10 time All Star and led the league in hitting in 1949 with an average of .343. That .343 average was a couple hundredths of a point higher than Ted Williams' .343. Williams would have won his third Triple Crown were it not for the final day of the season; Kell went 2 for 3 while Williams went 0 for 3. Kell led American League 3rd basemen in fielding average six times. He led the American League in hits and doubles in 1950 and 1951.

During his 15 year career Kell played for five teams which was rare for a marquee player of the era. In 1983 George Kell was elected into the Hall of Fame by the Veterans Committee.

Mace Brown on Hall of Famer Pie Traynor:

I liked playing for Pie Traynor
he was low keyed and never got on
the players.
              Best Wishes,
                Mace Brown

I liked playing for Pie Traynor he was low keyed and never got on the players.

Best Wishes,
Mace Brown

Mace Stanley Brown was born in North English Iowa in 1909. He joined the Pittsburgh Pirates in 1935 and pitched a decade in the Majors for the Pirates and the Red Sox with a brief stop in Brooklyn. Primarily a relief pitcher, Brown Led the National League with 51 appearances in 1938 and the American League with 49 appearances in 1943. His performance in the 1938 season earned him a National League All Star nod. Brown posted a career mark of 76 wins against 55 losses good for a .571 winning percentage. Of his 387 games pitched 332 were in relief.

For his brilliance as a 3rd baseman for 17 seasons with the Pittsburgh Pirates Pie Traynor was enshrined at the Baseball Hall of Fame in Cooperstown in 1948.

He managed the Pirates for six seasons from 1934 through 1939. In 1934, '35 and '37 he was a player manager. Traynor's .530 winning percentage bested his .320 career batting average but was not good enough to earn the Pennant for the Pirates.

Ed Fitz Gerald on Honus Wagner:

He always told the players to play hard and keep it clean. He was a great story teller too. He was with the Pirates all 5 years that I played for them.

He always talked to the players from the visiting teams too. They the I visitors had to come through our dug out to get on the field. They would always stop and talk to him.

Ed Fitz Gerald

He always told the players to play hard and keep it clean. He was a great story teller too. He was with the Pirates all 5 years that I played for them.

He always talked to the players from the visiting teams too. They, the visitors, had to come through our dug out to get on the field. They would always stop and talk to him.

Ed Fitz Gerald

Edward Raymond Fitz Gerald was born in Santa Ynez California in 1924. He went on to catch 651 Big League games over twelve seasons starting in 1948. Fitz Gerald spent time with the Pittsburgh Pirates, the Washington Senators and wrapped up with 49 games with the Cleveland Indians.

Honus Wagner's final season was 1917 however to this day he is in the discussion as the greatest shortstop to ever tread a diamond. The offensive categories he led the National League in during his 21 seasons would take up more room than we have here.

A quick rundown however still reveals what Wagner meant to the Big Leagues. His career batting average was .328 which accounted for his 3420 hits. At some point in his career he led the National League in every offensive category save home runs. Even so Wagner belted 101 home runs which was a prodigious amount during the dead ball era. Perhaps the most telling monument to Honus Wagner's esteem in the game is that he was immortalized in the inaugural class of the Baseball Hall Of Fame in Cooperstown NY in 1936.

Jim Greengrass on Rogers Hornsby:

He Was Great and all he
asked players to do was give 100%
of their ability. A Great hitter and
a fine Coach. The Greatest right hand
hitter of all time. Ted Williams was
the Greatest left hand hitter.
I played till my left leg gave out

Sincerely yours.
Jim

It was great and all he asked players to do was give 100% of their ability. A great hitter and fine coach. The greatest right handed hitter of all time. Ted Williams was the greatest left handed hitter.

I played till my left leg gave out.

Sincerely yours,
Jim

James Raymond Greengrass was born in Addison, NY in 1927. In 1952 he had an 18 game cup of coffee with the Cincinnati Reds. The following season Greengrass played a full 154 game season for the Reds and amassed 606 plate appearances. He used those appearances to hit .285, drive in 100 runs and slam 20 round trippers.

The following season Greengrass hit 27 homers and drove in 95 runs and batting .280. Those two seasons were the only two that he was healthy enough to play 139 games or more.

Over his five seasons in the Major Leagues Jim Greengrass played in 504 games. He used that time to amass 482 hits, 69 of which were home runs. That total along with his 82 doubles and 16 triples allowed him to slug for a .448 percentage.

Bobby Doerr on Satchel Paige:

Satchel Page never one of the great pitchers of baseball! I got. He saw him when I was 12 in Los Angeles pitch against a team my brother played on. Remember how fast he threw and how easy he made it look.

1948 hit against him when he was with Clev. He had lost the good fast ball, but great control, called hit the actual norm all day. Baldwin

ROBERT PERSHING DOERR
BOSTON, A.L. 1937-1951

NATIONAL BASEBALL HALL OF FAME & MUSEUM
Cooperstown, New York

Satchel Paige was one of the great pitchers of baseball. I got to see him when I was 12 in Los Angeles pitch against a team my brother played on. Remember how fast he was then and how easy he made it look.

1948 hit grand slam when he was with Cleve. He had lost the good fast ball but great control, could hit the outside corner all day.

Bob Doerr

Robert Pershing Doerr was born in Los Angeles California in 1918. He began his 14 year career in 1937. Doerr's entire tenure was spent playing his home games in Fenway Park with the Boston Red Sox. Doerr played exclusively at second base for the Sox and led the American League in fielding percentage for four seasons.

Bobby Doerr was excellent with his glove, but he really excelled at the plate. Most second basemen in the thirties and forties did not do what Doerr was able to do. During that era, second basemen were light with the bat and strong in the field.

Doerr was an anomaly as a power hitting second baseman. In 1944 he led the American League with a .528 slugging percentage. Six seasons Doerr topped one hundred runs batted in and in ten seasons he hit 15 or more homers.

The Hall Of Fame welcomed Bobby Doerr in 1986. His nine All Star nods at second base certainly warranted induction as did 223 round trippers and 1247 runs batted in from a traditionally weak offensive position.

Ernie Koy on Hall of Famer Leo Durocher:

Dear Craig:

Nice note

① When Leo joined the Dodgers we got along good

② On a fly ball to shallow left field. I was in left. Leo at short stop 2 was in left. Leo came out and called for the Pop fly.

③ Leo came out and called for the Pop fly. I stopped + Leo let the ball fall for a hit.

④ The had words (Bad words) that was the end of our Pal ship.

⑤ He like Medwick + traded for him - I was enclucled - so that was the end   good Luck

Hope this helps

Ernie Koy

Dear Craig:

> *Nice Note*
> *When Leo joined the Dodgers we got along good*
> *On a fly ball to shallow left field, I was in left. Leo at short*

stop.

> *Leo came out and called for the pop fly. I stopped & Leo let*

the ball fall for a hit.

> *We had words (bad words) that was the end of our pal ship.*
> *He liked Medwick & traded for him- I was included- so that*

was the end.

> *Good luck*
> *Hope this helps*
> *Ernie Koy*

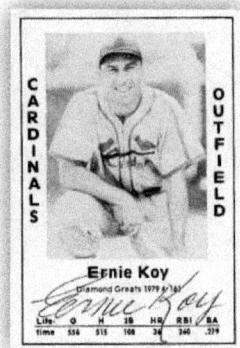

Ernie Koy played five years in the Big Leagues. As his note mentions, he was included in a trade mid season in 1940 to St. Louis for Hall of Famer Ducky Medwick. Koy had a .279 lifetime average with 515 hits including 36 home runs.

Ernie spent time on the grid iron as a fullback for the University of Texas 1930-'32. His sons Ernie Jr. and Ted played on the National Championship Longhorns teams. Ernie Jr. in 1963 and Ted in 1969. Both sons also spent time in the National Football League.

Paul Hopkins on the state of the game:

Dear Graig,
about some of the
question's you asked for
Baseball has not changed
much as far as rules are
concerned
What has changed are
the operations of B.B. such
as the desire to let money
take over, owners want too
win + will pay any amount to
to get the best players +
then the players are for the
most part are not interested
in the game for the fun
of it, The best thing would be
to get a Comisoner who
loves B.B. + will have complete
control over the entire funchan
of being able to handle any problem
They are out there but the

Dear Craig,

    About some of the questions you asked for.

    Baseball has not changed much as far as rules are concerned.

    What has changed are the operations B.B. such as the desire to let money take over. Owners want to win & will pay any amount to get the best players & then the players are for the most part not interested in the game for the fun of it.

    The best thing would be to get a commissioner who loves B.B. & will have complete control over the entire function of being able to handle any problem they are out there but the owners lack the overall interest or guts to do what is needed and that is to get a commissioner.

    Sincerely,
    Paul Hopkins

    Paul Henry Hopkins was born in Chester, Connecticut in 1904. In his rookie year of 1927 as a member of the Washington Senators he gave up Babe Ruth's record tying 59th homer in his record setting 60 home run season. Hopkins pitched 11 games in two seasons with the Washington Senators and the St. Louis Cardinals. He started one of his eleven games with his other 10 appearances coming in relief. Paul Hopkins career Major League record reads one win against one loss with 11 strikeouts in 27.1 innings and a 2.96 earned run average.

Dave "Boo" Ferriss on cutting John Grisham:

My Biggest Coaching Mistake —

In the fall of 1974 nineteen year old John Grisham enrolled at Delta State after playing one season of baseball at Northwest Miss. Junior College. I was glad to give him the opportunity to be a walk-on in our fall practice.

John had a passion for baseball, a burning desire to be a professional baseball player. He had very little interest in academics and books, just wanted to play baseball. He was a hard worker and gave 100% effort every day.

We gave John a good look in our practice sessions as we did all walk-ons. He worked hard but we didn't think he had the ability to make our squad.

It was tough for me to tell him that we couldn't keep him, suggesting he stay at Delta State and concentrate on his studies. He showed no interest in doing this as books were not his first love by any means.

I've always told John he made a big mistake by not telling me that one day he would be famous. Knowing this I believe I would have found a place for him, maybe help me coach or get in the lineup when we are way ahead. There would be visions of him supplying the funds someday for a retractable roof for our field — could have named it the Grisham Dome. No such luck!

At the end of the fall term he and his two close friends transferred to Miss. State University. He says he finally waked up one day and decided he needed to forget baseball and pay attention to his books. You know the rest of the story as he went on to become one of our greatest authors.

In February 2008 he initiated an athletic fund raising event, primarily for our baseball program, on our campus. We had a huge turnout and $130,000 was raised in the one evening, a wonderful and delightful affair.

John is evermore a fine person, a down-to-earth and humble fellow, and has been more than generous in giving back to his home state. Near his Virginia home he has built seven baseball and softball fields where over 500 youngsters play every summer.

John didn't make his mark in playing the game, but he has never lost his love and passion for the game. He is a great American and has made us proud. Oh, if he had just told me that someday he would be famous !!!

Dave "Boo" Ferriss

My Biggest Coaching Mistake-

In the fall of 1974 nineteen year old John Grisham enrolled at Delta State after playing one season of baseball at Northwest Miss. Junior College. I was glad to give him the opportunity to be a walk-on in our fall practice.

John had a passion for baseball, a burning desire to be a professional baseball player. He had very little interest in academics and books, just wanted to play baseball. He was a hard worker and gave 100% effort every day. We gave John a good look in our practice sessions as we did all walk-ons. He worked hard but we didn't think he had the ability to make our squad.

It was tough for me to tell him that we couldn't keep him, suggesting he stay at Delta State and concentrate on his studies. He showed no interest in doing this as books were not his first love by any means.

I've always told John he made a big mistake by not telling me that one day he would be famous. Knowing this I believe I would have found a place for him, maybe help me coach or get in the lineup when we are way ahead. There would be visions of him supplying the funds someday for a retractable roof for our field- could have named it the Grisham Dome. No such luck!

At the end of the fall term he and his two close friends transferred to Miss. State University. He says he finally woke up one day and decided he needed to forget baseball and pay attention to his books. You know the rest of the story as he went on to become one of our greatest authors.

In February 2008 he initiated an athletic fund raising event, primarily for our baseball program on our campus. We had a huge turnout and $130,000 was raised in one evening, a wonderful and delightful affair.

John is evermore a fine person, a down-to-earth and humble fellow, and has been more than generous in giving back to his home state. Near his Virginia home he has built seven baseball and softball fields where over 500 youngsters play every summer.

John didn't make his name in playing the game, but he has never lost his love and passion for the game. He is a great American and has made us proud. Oh, if he had just told me that someday he would be famous!!!

Dave "Boo" Ferriss

Dave Meadow Ferriss was born in Shaw, Mississippi on the fifth day of December, 1921. After attending Mississippi State University and a stint in the military he debuted on the mound for the Boston Red Sox in 1945. Sox fans were treated to great production from their young hurler as Ferriss earned 21 wins against 10 losses in his rookie season. To prove his rookie season was not an aberration, Boo went 25 and six in his sophomore campaign while helping Boston to the American League Pennant. Boston lost the World Series to the St. Louis Cardinals in seven games with Ferriss going 1-0 in two starts. Arm injuries limited the rest of his career and his last appearance on the rubber was in 1950. Overall as a player Boo compiled 65 wins against 30 losses.

After a four seasons as pitching coach for the Red Sox, Ferriss went on to coach the Delta State Statesmen beginning in the 1960 season. In 26 seasons as coach at Delta State Ferriss compiled a 639-387 record. He has been inducted into the Halls of Fame of Delta State, Mississippi State, the American Baseball Coaches Association and Mississippi Sports. Boo is also a member of the Boston Red Sox Hall of Fame.

Marvin Miller on the reserve clause:

Annual Salaries in the Major Leagues in the years leading up to free agency approximated: minimum salary - $18,000; mean average salary - $34,000, maximum salary - $150,000.

Currently: minimum salary $327,000 (under the recent, new Agreement -- $380,000 in 2007 and $400,000 in 2008).

average salary -- over $2.5 million, top salary - $25.2 million.

[over the years the owners income from baseball has increased from $50 million (in 1967) to $5.2 <u>billion</u> this year.]

Unlike the inaccurate beliefs of many of those who have written and talked about player movement, the fact is that fewer players change teams from year to year in current years, than the number of major league players who were traded or sold to other teams in an average year in the past, before Free Agency.

M.

Marvin Miller

Craig Sievers

Annual salaries in the Major Leagues in the years leading up to free agency approximated: minimum salary-$18,000, mean average salary-$34,000, maximum salary-$150,000.

Currently: $327,000 (Under the recent new agreement $380,000 in 2007 and $400,000 in 2008) average salary over $2.5 million; top salary $25.2 million.

[Over the years the owners' revenue from baseball has far increased from $50 million (in 1967) to $5.2 billion this year.]

Unlike the inaccurate beliefs of many of those who have written and talked about player movement, the fact is that fewer free aganet players change teams from year to year in current years than the number of Major League players who were traded or sold to other teams in an average year in the past, before free agency.

M.

Marvin Miller was an economist and one of the most influential figures in the history of Major League Baseball. Mr. Miller was the executive director of the Major League Baseball Players Association from 1966 through 1982. He created the Players Union and under his guidance it became one of the strongest labor unions in America. Mr. Miller negotiated the collective bargaining agreement to include independent arbitration. What that meant was that any contract dispute between a player and a team would be reviewed by a person outside of the league. Before this time, disputes would be sent to the Commissioner. Of course the Commissioner was selected by the owners so the players were at a disadvantage. It is widely agreed that Marvin Miller should have long ago been enshrined at Cooperstown.

Craig Sievers on this book:

Thank you for reading my book
I hope you enjoyed it.
All the biographical information
on the pages previous was gleaned
from The 2005 ESPN Baseball
Encyclopedia, the backs of old
baseball cards and from stories
I remember from who knows
where. I cleaned up some dates
and details using wikipedia.
If you have any disagreements
with any of the stats or whatnot
feel free to write me a letter.

Sincerely,

Craig

Craig Sievers was born in Fort Collins, Colorado in 1980. He moved to New York in 2004 and has resided in Auburn, NY since 2006. Sievers is an unwavering Denver Broncos fan and his autograph collection encompassing all sports is ever growing. In his free time he enjoys golfing when the western New York weather permits and spends time at Downtown Books & Coffee in Auburn. Having travelled rather extensively, Viet Nam, Honduras, Mexico and Japan are among the stamps on Craig's passport. He is a skilled craftsman, tile mason and painter. Those traits allow him to make his living as a maintenance man.